FTC COMPLIANCE GUIDE

DON'T SAY THAT

HOW TO ADVERTISE WITHOUT GETTING SUED BY THE FTC & OTHER AGENCIES

Greg Christiansen, ESQ. & Anik Singal

DON'T SAY THAT

Copyright @2024 by Greg Christiansen & Anik Singal

All rights reserved. No part of this publication may be reproduced, distributed, or transmitted in any form or by any means, including photocopying, recording, or any other electronic or mechanical methods, without the prior written permission of the publisher, except in the case of brief quotations embodied in critical reviews and certain other noncommercial uses permitted by copyright law.

Table of Contents

Preface 1
Introduction 7

Part 1: The FTC, Laws, and Other Agencies 13
    Chapter 1: Who Is the FTC? 15
        The Main Responsibilities of the FTC 18
        The Long Arm of the FTC 21
        How Active Is the FTC? 22
        Is the FTC the Only Thing to Worry About? 22
        Marketer's Perspective 23
    Chapter 2: Other Agencies 25
        Federal Communications Commission 25
        State Regulatory Bodies 28
        The Better Business Bureau (BBB) 31
        American Association of Retired Persons 32
    Chapter 3: Key Industries Tracked 35
    Chapter 4: The Three Most Common Federal Laws the FTC Uses 49
        Section 5 50
        Section 13(b) 54
        Section 19 56

Part 2: The Cost of Not Complying 59
    Chapter 5: "This Won't Happen to Me" 61
        Common Myths 61
    Chapter 6: How FTC Enforcement Has Changed 67
        Notice of Penalty Offenses 67
        Section 13(b) & Section 19 68
        Marketer's Perspective 69

Chapter 7: What It Costs to Be Investigated 71
    The Lawyers 72
    The Discovery 72
    The Fine 74
    Loss of Business Opportunities 75
    Why Settle & Not Just Go To Court? 76
    Lawyer's Perspective 77
Chapter 8: The Non-Monetary Cost of Being Investigated 79
    Health 81
    Reputation Damage 82
    Banking Challenges 82
    Injunctions & Bans 83
    Lawyer's Perspective 84
Chapter 9: How Do I Stay Off the Radar? 87
    Complaints 88
    Business Associates 89
    State-Level Investigations 91
    Past Cases & Business Partners 91
    Noncompliant Marketing 92
    Marketer's Perspective 93
Chapter 10: An Overview of the Investigative Process 95
    Internal Investigation 95
    Warning Letter 96
    CID 97
    Lawsuit, TRO, Asset Freeze 97
    Settlement or Lawsuit 98
    Injunctive Relief 98
    Press Release 99
    Customer Notification 99
    Marketer's Perspective 100

Part 3: How To Comply 101
Chapter 11: Breaking Down The Rules 103
    Marketer's Perspective 105
Chapter 12: Misrepresentations 107
    Marketer's Perspective 116

- Chapter 13: It All Starts & Ends with "Net Impression" 117
  - Marketer's Perspective 122
- Chapter 14: Earnings Claims 123
  - What if I CAN Back Up My Claim? 132
  - Marketer's Perspective 133
- Chapter 15: Substantiation 137
  - Absolute Statements 141
  - General Statements 143
  - How Do You Get Substantiation? 143
  - Lawyer's Perspective 146
- Chapter 16: Testimonials 146
  - How Can I Use Testimonials? 154
  - Marketer's Perspective 156
- Chapter 17: Goal-Setting 159
  - Marketer's Perspective 163
- Chapter 18: Selectivity, Qualification, & Scarcity 165
  - False Scarcity 166
  - Fake Qualification 168
  - Qualifying Related Red Flags 170
  - Marketer's Perspective 171
- Chapter 19: Refunds & Guarantees 173
  - Special Class of Customers To Refund Even Faster 174
  - A Refund Period is MANDATORY—Cooling Off Period 175
  - Marketer's Perspective 177
- Chapter 20: Value Stacking 179
  - Comparison Selling 180
  - Marketer's Perspective 182
- Chapter 21: Key Phrases To Avoid 185
  - Marketer's Perspective 193
- Chapter 22: Written-Sales Page Violations 195
  - The Terms of Services Pages 195
  - Privacy Policy Pages 197
  - Contact Information 198
  - Marketer's Perspective 199
- Chapter 23: Webinars & Video Sales Letters 201
  - Marketer's Perspective 208

Chapter 24: Tele-Sales Violations 211
    Marketer's Perspective 217
Chapter 25: Recurring Sales Violations 219
    Marketer's Perspective 222

Conclusion 225
Appendix: Important Cases 229

Preface

Anik Singal

My attorney called, and I clicked "decline."

"I'll get back to him later," I thought.

Within ten seconds, he called again.

"Uh-oh…"

If your attorney calls you twice back-to-back, you pretty much know you're in trouble.

I dropped whatever I was doing and was just about to call him back, when suddenly, there was a knock on my office. Lisa, our office assistant, walked in with a FedEx package. I don't know why or how, but something inside me immediately knew what was happening. My heart fell to the bottom of my stomach, even before the package was handed to me.

My face got warm. A wave of fear swept over me.

There it was.

The package said "Federal Trade Commission" right across the top; a "gift" from the government that no one ever wants.

Now, I'm no stranger to stress. I've been in business for 21 years, near bankruptcy twice. I've gone through many economies. I've seen good days. I've seen bad days. But that particular day was one of the worst.

As I read the 31-page audit report, I could tell that they had been thoroughly reviewing my work, possibly for years. I couldn't understand. As far as I knew, I was compliant. I had a large law firm on my side. But as compliant as I thought I was, and as good as I'd been to my customers, I suddenly realized that I was in for a long and painful ride.

One that would end up costing me millions of dollars and a lifetime of PTSD.

I was offended. I was triggered. I went into full-blown fight mode, nearly screaming at the document while I read it.

"Stop saying that! That's completely untrue!" I argued, with no one there to hear me. I had a refund rate that was far lower than the industry average and a chargeback rate that was almost nonexistent. I had an A rating at the BBB. I had never been sued. I had a great reputation, happy customers, vendors, partners, you name it.

So, what was the problem?

Unfortunately, the Federal Trade Commission (FTC) didn't care about any of those things. They were solely focused on the language I was using in my sales material; down to specific words and sentences, some even from presentations I had stopped using years ago.

Intention be damned. Reputation be damned. What I was about to learn was that the law is the law, and it couldn't care less about your intention. Those words I used in my sales material were enough to put me in the middle of an investigation. In the beginning, it really felt like they were

Preface

coming after me like I was some Don from the underworld. Anik Corleone, "the Godfather."

The reality was that I didn't even know what I was doing was wrong. If I had, I would have fixed it. I was always taught that, if your customers aren't complaining, you're good. If you just build a good service, the FTC won't need to look at you.

And I did all that.

We had amazing customer stats, even after 60,000+ transactions in just 3 years. I had invested millions in my customer care.

But...

Sometimes you don't know what you don't know. And the fact is that ignorance is not a defense. It doesn't matter if you didn't know you were violating the law; in the FTC's eyes a violation is a violation.

The FTC investigation was the worst experience of my life. Yes, even worse than the time I nearly died from disease and surgery. I spent one particular year of my life battling and nearly dying from Crohn's Disease. Back in 2005, I was in the ICU for three months, getting two pints of blood transfused into me daily.

I lost the ability to even sit up straight. I was laid out flat with nothing but pain to keep me company. For more than 90 days, my heart rate would spike at the slightest movement. I was flat for so long, my leg muscles completely eroded.

I eventually had to go through a nearly 10-hour surgery with the doctors worrying as to whether I would even survive. It was nothing short of a miracle that I did survive, but my pain wasn't over yet.

After surgery, I had to build a make-shift hospital in my parent's basement. It took me two months of physical therapy just to learn to walk again. Then, six months later, I needed surgery again. Then, two weeks after that surgery, I was admitted in the hospital again for another month and ended up needing another major surgery.

It was hell.

It took me a year to be healthy enough to enter back into society. Sounds bad right?

Being investigated by the FTC was worse. Far worse. The physical harm I had suffered in sickness was no match for the mental anguish I suffered during my FTC investigation.

Yes, I just said that being investigated by the government was worse than losing the ability to walk, having multiple surgeries, and nearly dying. And I mean it.

Don't do what I did and assume that things like customer service, low refunds, and a good reputation will shield you from investigation. Don't *ever* think that you're too small or too new, or because your business is in a foreign country, you are exempt from the ever reaching arm of the FTC or another regulatory body. The FTC is indiscriminate. There are countless actions brought against small businesses, medium businesses, large businesses, completely new businesses, international businesses, and non-citizens.

Don't put off dealing with it until it's too late.

Your single best defense is "Knowledge." If I had known then what I know now, I would have avoided so much pain. Armor up with knowledge, and play the game within the rules. Anything else isn't worth it. There isn't a cost I wouldn't have paid to avoid my experience with the FTC.

You don't want to get a similar package from the FTC, trust me. It was the beginning of a whole lot of pain that could have been avoided.

Let me tell you how…

Introduction

Greg Christiansen

Anik was referred to me by a long-term client. The first time we spoke, he had reached out to me only hours after receiving an investigative demand from the FTC. He was incredibly stressed, and I could tell he was in shock. At that point, I really didn't know much about Anik or his company, Lurn. Calls like this are difficult because you recognize that, once the demand from the FTC is made, it is generally not a matter of if, but of when and how much. I empathized with Anik's pain because you could tell he genuinely loved his company and respected his clients.

Unfortunately, Anik's call was not unique. I've had many similar calls over the years. I generally ask a lot of questions and do a lot of listening during these initial conversations. When I first started my practice, low consumer complaints and low chargebacks were a great indicator that a company was complying with the law. Yet as I listened to Anik, I could sense his frustration that something like this could happen to him despite all of the support he'd provided his clients. I could also tell he was facing a huge uphill battle.

Our first conversation was on a Friday night. We talked for two hours that night, and then three more the following Sunday. When I'm talking to a client who already has representation, I generally support their existing counsel. Since Anik had representation, I just did a lot of listening and started recommending some small changes to help eliminate some of the bigger issues I had identified.

After I hung up, I really didn't expect to hear from Anik again. To my surprise, he called me a few weeks later. He wanted a second opinion and asked if I'd fly out to Maryland to meet with him and his team in person to audit their marketing material and sales calls.

After spending two days with his team, I was pleased to see that, for the most part, they had done an excellent job. It was far better than what I normally see. Yet I realized there were some nuances to compliance that he just didn't know.

I identified the problems almost immediately.

After reviewing his marketing and telephone calls, I could see why they were in legal trouble. Specifically, I identified the four key words that I believed would become the focus of the case. What were those four words? I'll spell them out later in the book. For now, it's enough to know that those four words were the last ones Anik ever expected to cause him harm. I'm not saying that was the only issue with his marketing. I'm just saying that I had predicted what would go on to become the primary issue of the case (and it turns out I was right).

Anik was shocked.

Initially, he didn't believe me and wanted to know how I was able to narrow the entire case down to just those four words. My answer was simple. I told him, "I just live in the weeds on this stuff. These types of cases have a lot of repetition in them. If you study enough of them, it's not hard to stay out of trouble."

I'm not a prophet. Good attorney's, like a good detective, watch for the signs. And that starts with identifying and knowing the trends and the rules.

Months later, as the investigation came to an end, there we were, almost exactly where I predicted just eight months earlier. Those four words had reared their ugly head to become the central focus of the case.

Over the duration of the investigation, Anik and I spent hours together. I marveled at how his questions went from "*why did this happen*" to "*how did this happen.*" He was like a mad scientist, completely dedicated to dissecting the reason this happened to him.

Anik was serious about understanding what mistakes he made. Generally, when I assist with settling an action, clients are outraged and upset. They are rarely introspective. Yet here was a client in the middle of the storm, genuinely holding himself accountable and wanting to do better.

He piqued my interest.

Today, with his case settled and behind us, I find myself speaking on a lot of stages with Anik. I'm amazed at how open he is. Anik has made it his mission to "*spread the good news of compliance,*" as he calls it.

His opinion, and my experience, is that most business owners are honest, good people, and they're happy to be compliant. They just don't understand the laws. Or they jump the gun and assume what the law means. They "model" what others are doing and just assume that the practices must be legal.

The truth is that the company they are modeling most likely bumped the legal review and has fallen into a compliance trap. It always shocks me how little preparation marketers do or how little legal advice they get prior to launching their products and campaigns.

Or, worse yet, they do get advice they don't like and quickly give up, falsely assuming that compliant marketing will never convert. But I'm here to tell you that I have several successful clients who get amazing results, all using compliant marketing. It's my hope that Anik and I are able to help show you how to do exactly that.

For me, it's been almost 20 years. I live and breathe these rules, and I love helping companies with their compliance. It's a true honor.

From day one I've loved being in the trenches. My journey after law school began as a clerk in the Nevada Supreme Court. I wanted direct access, an upfront view of the evaluation of arguments and argument styles from a judge's perspective. For a full year, I gained an invaluable education working on the front lines of our legal system.

After completing my clerkship, I returned to my hometown, Salt Lake City, Utah. My best friend and I, both Jesuit law school alumni from opposite sides of the country, decided to start a law practice together. Initially, we cast a wide net, taking various types of work. Our first significant case was a publicly traded company in Utah that was facing a regulatory issue with the State. They'd hired a big law firm to handle the lawsuit but wanted us, as the younger boutique firm, to manage all the grunt work. Naively, we jumped in, handling depositions and other behind-the-scenes tasks leading up to the trial.

On the eve of the trial, the large law firm representing the company unexpectedly refused to do anything other than opening and closing arguments. The company's CEO and president approached us, acknowledging our hands-on experience in the case, and asked if we'd tackle the litigation. Despite feelings of inadequacy, we accepted the challenge. The case had millions of dollars on the line, and the pressure was immense.

The administrative proceedings went as expected, and we lost. Like in most regulatory matters, the deck is usually stacked against the Defendant (you). In this case, the state had several attorneys who were arguing their case in front of an administrative law judge, who also worked for the state. In other words, it wasn't exactly an impartial venue.

The only saving grace is that appeals were heard *de novo*, which meant that we could get a review for appeals without any influence from the ruling. Obviously, we appealed. We also filed a federal action against the State of Utah. I'll spare you the legal reasons, but essentially our purpose was not to obtain damages from the State of Utah. Instead, we wanted to encourage settlement.

The strategy paid off. By pushing to sue the state and the individuals involved, we compelled the state to settle for approximately $250,000. Ultimately, this publicly traded company replaced their in-house counsel with me.

Over the following three years, I crisscrossed the United States, assisting in settling and litigating 23 lawsuits in various states. This period marked the beginning of my legal practice in marketing and advertising. For the past two decades, my focus has revolved around assisting companies in pinpointing issues in their marketing methods.

I've worked extensively with various individuals and companies in this space. For me, marketing is creativity. The problem with most marketers, however, is that they take shortcuts. They want fast results that generally come at the expense of sacrificing compliance. The irony in this is that there is a perfectly legal way to do most marketing. The key is to provide transparency, allowing the client to understand exactly what they are getting for their money.

The clients I work best with freely communicate with me about their marketing methods. For example, Anik's gotten into the habit of texting me before hitting "publish" on any web content. I provide this service for my clients, and through this book, I hope you may learn some of the techniques and skills I teach my clients.

When working with clients like Anik, the goal is to allow them to remain within the letter of the law but still convert incredibly well (sometimes even better than before). Marketing is fun. It's about being clever and smart. Complying with the law doesn't mean you have to give up all your strategies. You just need to refine them so that they appeal to customers without misleading them.

The purpose of this book is education.

I believe my primary role as an attorney is to train clients to think like me when creating their advertising materials. We are both genuinely interested in helping people avoid the kind of heartache Anik had to deal with. If publishing this book loses me a client or two because they manage to avoid landing on the FTC's radar, I'm perfectly okay with that.

After seeing so many people go through the long, drawn out process that regulators put companies through, I can safely say it's something you don't want to experience for yourself.

Ever.

Part 1:
The FTC, Laws, and Other Agencies

Chapter 1:
Who Is the FTC?

Greg Christiansen

The year was 1914. World War I just started, and Woodrow Wilson was President. Congress introduced income tax for the first time. American Tobacco was charging what seemed like a fortune for cigarettes and could get away with it because they had a monopoly over the industry. Standard Oil, headed by John D. Rockefeller, did the same thing for the oil industry. During this era, big industry was out of control, utilizing ruthless practices, and the public wanted to put a stop to it.

Enter the Sherman Antitrust Act.

In 1890, Congress passed the Sherman Antitrust Act. The "Sherman Act," as it was called, was created with the purpose of breaking down the big monopolies and creating an even playing field for small business owners to compete. The intention was to eliminate large businesses from "scheming" together as "trusts" to stifle competition and increase their profits. Unfortunately, the Sherman Act didn't have enough teeth in its initial terms to deter businesses from blatantly violating its provisions.

Congress realized it lacked the authority to protect consumers from many of the violations of the Sherman Act. So, in 1914, they enacted two additional Antitrust legislations, the Clayton Act and the Federal Trade Commission (FTC) Act.

The Clayton Act addresses specific practices that the Sherman Act does not clearly prohibit, such "as mergers and interlocking directorates (that is, the same person making business decisions for competing companies)." The FTC Act is a consumer and business regulation that prohibits "unfair methods of competition" and "unfair or deceptive acts or practices."

The FTC Act included provisions to stop, and in some cases, reimburse clients who were misled or who purchased a product or service based on deceptive representations. With the FTC Act, the FTC was born. Its charter, however, not only regulated monopolies, but also created safety provisions for clients who purchased variable products and services.

Over the years, the FTC has added clarifications, rules, guidance, and amendments to supplement its authority, including the Telemarketing Sales Rule, the Pay-Per-Call Rule, and the Equal Credit Opportunity Act. It became one of the primary methods the government used to protect consumers as technology and sales techniques developed.

In the late 1940s and early 1950s, print, radio, and television commercials became increasingly aggressive, making claims such as "More doctors smoke Camels." Remember the Marlboro Man? Cowboy hat, horse, a reflection of a true man, he made smoking seem cool. Well, now that we know how bad smoking is, let me ask you a question.

When was the last time you saw a person smoking a cigarette in a commercial?

Selling cigarettes on TV doesn't happen anymore. The FTC and the Surgeon General's office decided that it was a negative promotion, meaning that they were promoting a product that caused lung damage and drastically raised the cost of healthcare across the country. That led to the ban on cigarette advertisements on television.

In the late 1970s, there was a push to control what marketing companies said in their ads. Ralph Nader and his group, Nader's Raiders, were a big part of that. Nader was a politician most famous for running against Al Gore in 2000 on the Green Party ticket. He got together a group of seven volunteer law students and investigated the FTC for their part in allowing unsafe cars to stay on the road. This was after Nader published a book called *Unsafe at Any Speed*, which was a critique of the American Auto Industry, and GM in particular.

After the investigation, there was an overhaul at the FTC, leading to a lot more scrutiny of companies that weren't in compliance. Basically, Nader was saying, "Hey, we're paying attention. You better do your job and hold these companies accountable."

In the 1980s, infomercials began, followed by ads from home shopping networks. Anyone who still watches television should be familiar with these 30-minute ads for anything from weight loss supplements to hair growth products. The FTC got involved when they realized that people didn't understand they were ads. People genuinely believed them to be television shows featuring good hearted "folks" who were just sharing information out of the goodness of their hearts. The FTC cracked down, forcing marketers to disclose that this programming was paid advertising that was meant to sell a product.

As the internet became popular in the early 1990s, it opened up a whole new world. One of the initial cases brought by the FTC regarding advertisements on the Internet was FTC v. Corizine. Corizine sold credit repair kits on AOL. The FTC said it was a case of a "traditional scam" moving to the Internet. So, they began their journey of dealing with internet marketers. Just five years later, they crossed the 100-case mark against online businesses.

The FTC actually started a practice called "surf days," where they got together with law enforcement agencies all across the country to sit around and surf the internet looking for dubious websites. Just think about hundreds of civil servants taking a full day to snoop around, looking for noncompliant marketing.

No matter what the product, service, or industry, the FTC's mission is:

> *"to protect the public from deceptive or unfair business practices and from unfair methods of competition through law enforcement, advocacy, research, and education."*

It's a necessary part of the business field, but it can, at times, also come down hard on companies that don't always deserve it. It's not uncommon for there to be friendly fire. Because the FTC's interpretation of the law is not always discernible, a lot of companies get caught in the cross-fire. That's why we're writing this book. We want you to understand the FTC, how it works, some of their basic interpretations of marketing practices, how to avoid as many pitfalls as possible, and most importantly, how to stay off their radar.

The Main Responsibilities of the FTC

The FTC has developed into a powerful consumer protection agency, with the primary goal of stopping consumers from getting "fleeced." They'll use a bunch of different words, including "misleading," "deceptive," "fraud," "scammed," "ripped off," and "robbed." Without all the drama, there are three main responsibilities of the current FTC that relate to telemarketing activity and internet marketing.

1. Advertising Laws

Section 5 of the FTC Act is a deceptive trade practices provision. Basically, it sets forth the FTC's core purpose of ensuring advertisements are truthful and don't contain express misrepresentations or create an improper "net impression." They have laws against false claims, bait-and-switch schemes, and unsubstantiated claims. You've probably seen false claims when it comes to many industries, such as:

- The "Ab Circle Pro," which made its rounds claiming one could lose "10 pounds in 2 weeks…"
- The endless "make $10,000 a month with your online business" ads…
- The "build wealth with no-cash-down real estate investing" ads…
- The "how to win 86% of your options trading" ads…

We're absolutely surrounded by these types of ads on Facebook, Instagram, TikTok, YouTube, and Google.

The niches I mention above are not the only problematic ones. Actually, the FTC is not limited to any particular niche at all. For example, in 2015, the FTC accused the department store Lord & Taylor of paying fashion influencers to make Instagram posts promoting their lines of clothing, without disclosing that these posts were actually part of a marketing campaign.

Basically, they gave a bunch of influencers the same dress, and people took pictures. But they also paid all those influencers, creating the impression that they were voluntarily promoting an item, when in fact, they were paid to do so.

> The FTC complaint charges Lord & Taylor with three separate violations: 1) that Lord & Taylor falsely represented that the 50 Instagram images and captions reflected the independent statements of impartial fashion influencers, when they really were part of a Lord & Taylor ad campaign to promote sales of its new line; 2 … Mar 15, 2016
>
> FTC Federal Trade Commission (.gov)
> https://www.ftc.gov › business-guidance › blog › 2016/03

Image Source: FTC (2016)[1]

---

[1] FTC. 2016. FTC's Lord & Taylor case: In native advertising, clear disclosure is always in style. https://www.ftc.gov/business-guidance/blog/2016/03/ftcs-lord-taylor-case-native-advertising-clear-disclosure-always-style

The store also paid a magazine to run an article that looked like a regular story, but was really a paid ad. In the eyes of the FTC, that is a big problem. Consumers must be able to distinguish between an advertisement and a news program. There has to be an upfront acknowledgement of the fact that you're selling something. Lord & Taylor settled with the FTC for $100,000. Not a significant sum in today's FTC settlements, but a noteworthy one as it pertains to truthful advertising.

In recent actions, the primary cause of investigation and litigation is the use of false and/or unsubstantiated claims. The consequences of violating advertising rules are getting more and more extreme by the day.

2. Privacy & Data Protection

With the advancement of the internet and the collection of credit card numbers, privacy and data protection are atop the list of FTC concerns. In 2019, the FTC fined Facebook $5 billion for privacy violations. Today, you can't buy a cup of coffee or purchase something at the grocery store without someone requesting your private information. Companies not only have names and contact information, but all kinds of data, including family connections, product preferences, places people visit, and so on.

In the Facebook case, it allegedly made it seem like consumers had control over their own information. They had privacy settings that didn't do much good. The company was still profiting from all the data they collected. The FTC intervened, and it cost Facebook a small fortune.

3. Overseeing Mergers & Acquisitions

The FTC's interest in Mergers & Acquisitions is a call back to yester years. In fact, it's pretty much why it was founded. The problem with monopolies is that when one company controls the product category on the market, they control the supply chain, the pricing, and everything else about the product, making the consumer completely beholden to them.

History is full of examples of the FTC stopping mergers that it believes will harm consumers. A recent example is the merger between Staples and Office Depot. As long as the two companies remain separate, the customer has a choice. But if they merge, then customers would only have the illusion of choice, which is a big problem.

The Long Arm of the FTC

The FTC has jurisdiction over both companies and individuals. In fact, when an investigation is launched, the FTC will almost always include the individual owners of the underlying companies. Most FTC cases involve the company, related companies, the founder, and others in key decision-making/manager positions. So, when Anik was investigated, the FTC not only investigated his company, but also investigated him personally.

Yes, this means that even a company's key employees may get wrapped up in an FTC case.

It also means that when the FTC investigates, it doesn't limit its scope of questioning to the business's activities, but also extends it to your individual actions, including your personal finances. They will often ask for a personal financial statement, often referred to as a "PFS."

When it came time to settle for Anik, the FTC wanted to know about his main company, Lurn, Inc., about all his other unrelated businesses, and of course, his personal finances. They wanted to know everything. It didn't matter whether or not a particular financial asset had anything to do with his business. If it had value, they were interested.

The FTC is very thorough when they conduct an investigation, and they'll cast their net as wide as they can. And you don't want to lie to the FTC. It'll just make things worse.

How Active Is the FTC?

If you want to understand how active the FTC is, we've got to look at their actions over time. The FTC publishes annual reports and has been doing so since 1916. The annual reports are presented to Congress every year and have detailed summaries of all their cases, collections, and rulings.

In recent years, the pace of the FTC's investigations has significantly increased. In 2021, the FTC filed 80 enforcement actions against companies for deceptive advertising and received 4.8 million consumer complaints. That was a 70% increase over 2020 in terms of complaints.

The FTC has also increased its staffing to keep up with the growing number of consumer complaints. In 2021, the FTC hired 250 new employees to work on consumer protection issues. Maybe it was the launch of the virtual workplace or just the increased reliance on internet advertising, but something's been pushing the FTC to expand its activities.

Is the FTC the Only Thing to Worry About?

The FTC is a heavy hitter in the field, but it's not the only regulatory agency you need to consider. Each state has its own laws, attorney generals who handle consumer complaints, and various acts that govern what you can or can't say. There has also been a big increase in consumer-led private lawsuits and class-actions.

Lastly, there are international regulations you have to take into account, and you may not even know it. Because commerce is worldwide, if you have any customers in any of the states or countries that have stricter laws, you have to pay attention. In the next chapter, we'll cover a few of the other organizations that are out there policing telesales and internet marketing.

Marketer's Perspective

Anik Singal

For 20 years, I stood on the sidelines and cheered on the FTC. I have seen them take down companies that were giving our industry a bad name, marketers that I felt were truly hurting people and hurting customers.

It wasn't until I got caught up in the trenches that I questioned the FTC. Yet even after having been through everything I went through, I still stand on the sidelines and believe in the work of and the need for an agency like the FTC. There are a lot of bad players out there, and if we don't have regulations, commerce is going to spiral into an anarchic disaster.

If I had my way, I might approach things a bit differently. I wouldn't attack anybody personally the way they do with their press releases (more on that later). I might give people a chance to change their ways before bringing down the hammer. I would be more specific in the warnings they issue, and I would work harder to decipher the players, not making it all black and white.

However, the rules are the rules, and it is what it is. If you want a change, vote!

In the end, even after having been sued by them, even after having lost a ton of sleep and a fortune, I still stand by the original purpose for which this organization was founded. I'm glad they're around. I just hope I never have to deal with them again.

Chapter 2:
Other Agencies

Greg Christiansen

The FTC is not the only game in town.

At the federal level, there's of course the FTC, but there are also other agencies that govern various forms of advertising and claims, like the Federal Communications Commission (FCC), the Food and Drug Administration (FDA), the Securities and Exchange Commission (SEC), and the Consumer Financial Protection Bureau (CFPB). In addition to federal regulatory bodies, you have non-regulatory institutions, such as the Better Business Bureau (BBB) and the American Association of Retired Persons (AARP), who can work directly with state and federal agencies.

Federal Communications Commission

The FCC is an agency that focuses on communications in the United States. It makes sure that telephone, radio, television, and internet are available to all Americans and investigates consumer complaints. The main difference between the FCC and the FTC is that the FCC focuses totally on communications, while the FTC is more involved with a wider range of advertising practices.

For example, in 2016, the FCC (not the FTC) fined AT&T $100 million for misleading customers about unlimited data plans. AT&T had been slowing down data speeds for customers who had unlimited data plans, which was a violation of the Open Internet Transparency Rule. In their opinion, unlimited was unlimited. There was no need for fine print letting customers know they were getting slower data. While the case could have potentially been tried by the FTC for the use of misleading ads, it was the FCC that took the lead because phone and internet come under their jurisdiction.

The FCC has a lot to say about telephone sales. For example, they enforce the Telephone Consumer Protection Act (TCPA), which was signed into law in 1991 and is most famous for the do-not-call registry, restrictions on robocalls, and laws about consent.

The TCPA has a lot of laws that are pretty specific. Things like you can only conduct a sales call between 8 am and 9 pm. Also, it requires every business to maintain a do-not-call list, in addition to following the national do-not-call registry. The TCPA also outlawed robocalls and unsolicited advertising faxes and is currently reviewing the use of ringless voicemails and artificial intelligence in telephone communications.

The main issue with the FCC and the TCPA is consent. Consent, consent, consent. In order to contact a client via telephone or text, you must have express written consent. That means when you're collecting their data, you need the written consent right there, visible and clear. Getting this written consent is an absolute defense against any violations. It's vital.

In December 2023, the FCC amended the TCPA to require companies obtaining consents to contact customers to expressly outline by whom and how they are consenting to be contacted. An example of an opt-in disclosure prior to December 2023 would read:

> *By providing your information today, you are giving consent for us or our partners to contact you by mail, phone, text, or email using automated technology based*

on the data provided, even if the phone number is present on a state or national Do-Not-Call list. You can do so in confidence, as we do not sell your personal information to other companies, and you can withdraw consent at any time. By submitting this form, you agree to our privacy policy and terms of service.

The problem with this pre-December 2023 opt-in language is that it creates a loop hole for marketers to obtain client information and then sell it to a third party, by using the term "us or our partners." The FCC's amendment of this provision now requires companies to obtain consent on a "one-on-one" basis. Under the new rule, you can only use the client's consent if it is specifically given and it's for a "logically and topically associated product and service."

What does this legal jargon mean? It means that if you want to get consent for your "partners," you have to obtain consent for your business and their business at the time of opt in. A new opt in would look like this:

By providing your information today, you are giving consent for us or our partners XYZ Corporation and ABC LLC to contact you by mail, phone, text or email using automated technology based on the data provided, even if the phone number is present on a state or national Do-Not-Call list. You can do so in confidence, as we do not sell your personal information to other companies, and you can withdraw consent at any time. By submitting this form, you agree to our privacy policy and terms of service.

Logical and topically associated products and services would be like this. If you were selling a weight loss product with a trainer or coach, the trainer or coach could contact the customer without violating the new TCPA regulations. However, if you were obtaining consent from a consumer to provide information about loan shopping, that would not allow you to contact the consumer to discuss loan consolidation, which is a completely different service.

As mentioned earlier, while the FCC and FTC are separate regulatory bodies that generally do their own thing, at times, they play together. On January 2, 2024, the FTC brought an action against Response Tree, LLC, a California-based "lead generator" company. As alleged by the FTC in its complaint, Response Tree operated more than 50 websites designed to obtain customer data. Response Tree then sold this data to various third-party companies, who then offered various products and services to the underlying customers. The FTC sued based on the allegation that these calls, which were made by robocalls and calls "to numbers on the DNC Registry, were illegal, as the telemarketers did not have consumers' consent to be called."

State Regulatory Bodies

Dealing with the federal government is like picking a fight with a 5,000-pound gorilla. Their scope, jurisdiction, authority, and resources span across the United States. In other words, they're very powerful, and they use that power. The FTC is known to do preliminary injunctions and asset freezes. The positioning of the FTC can be pretty extreme at times because they have the power to back it up.

The reach of a state regulatory body is generally limited to that state, unless it's where your business is based out of. Judgements by state regulatory bodies are generally only effective in the state itself, but they can be domesticated in other states as well.

I will often hear a client say, "Oh, it doesn't matter if the state comes after me because it's not the FTC." That is like saying you would rather take on the 3,000-pound gorilla, rather than the 5,000-pound one. The problem with that logic is that both gorillas are big enough to rip your arms off and beat you to death with them.

You see, the state and federal regulatory bodies don't exactly play fair. When a regulatory body brings an action, they spend months or even years preparing. When you get notice, you have maybe 20 to 30 days to respond. While you may have significant resources to apply to legal defense, the government has almost infinite resources to pull from. While you're fighting them with one or two attorneys, they're fighting you with four to five attorneys. It'll always be a dog fight right from the get go.

I'm not saying you can't put up a good fight. I certainly have, at times. But if we're being blunt, you have a government agency, in front of a government attorney, arguing in front of a government appointed judge. Who do you think has the advantage here?

You need to go no further than to look at the *FTC v. AMG Capital Management* case, which we'll discuss later in more detail. If you do your research, you'll see that for more than 40 years, motion grants and even judgments being handed down by the FTC have been based on a law that, in 2021, we discovered never really gave the FTC the authority to do so.

For 40 years that law never got challenged!

Fighting against a state is no laughing matter, either. It takes time, dedication, and significant resources. Even worse is when a state teams up with the FTC. In this case, I tell my clients to prepare for all out war.

Most state consumer protection divisions are operated and managed by the Attorney General's Office. Some states, like Utah, have a Division of Consumer Protection, which is governed by the state's Department of Commerce. Regulation is not always limited, however, to the state level. For example, in California, counties have their own regulatory and consumer protection bureaus. This now means that even District Attorneys can come after you.

The most common state regulatory laws include:

- A deceptive practices act
- A telemarketing solicitations act
- A business opportunity or seller assisted marketing plan act

Some states have more than these, but this always serves as a good starting point.

So the federal government sets the minimum laws and regulations. States cannot go below the federal regulations, but they're free to be more extreme. For example, federal law prohibits drinking alcohol before the age of 21. A state can raise the age to 25, but they cannot drop it to 18.

Here's some examples:

- In Montana, telemarketers have to be registered, or they'll face fines and even imprisonment.
- In California, you have to allow a client to opt out of consent in the same manner in which they opted in. This means that, if they bought a subscription plan online, they have to be able to cancel it online.
- In New York, you could face more than $50,000 in fines if you call a client to solicit services after 9:00 pm, EST.
- Many states have a rule that you have to provide a "cooling off period" of five or seven days, even though the federal government says 3 days.

Understanding state law is as important as understanding federal law. And you need to make sure you're compliant with the laws in every state in which you operate, regardless of where you're based.

The Better Business Bureau (BBB)

The mission of the BBB is to "promote marketplace trust." They provide a third-party system for consumers to publicly lodge complaints and for the business to publicly respond and resolve. The BBB is not a government regulatory body. It is a privately run business. The BBB was founded in 1912 after several high-profile scams. At the time, there were plenty of businesses using false advertising, bait-and-switch, and pyramid schemes.

For example, take Charles Ponzi and his "crime of the century." Around the time the BBB was established, Ponzi made millions by recruiting investors to recruit other investors. The BBB was established as a way for consumers to fight back against such scams and bring transparency to the marketplace.

The BBB is established as independent charters, geographically categorized. In theory, this was supposed to work very well. However, it has created challenges at times. Yet I have found most chapter presidents to be pretty agreeable and fair to companies when it comes to resolving problems and closing disputes. This is not always the case, but for the most part, your company should feel comfortable developing a healthy relationship with your BBB charter and working with them to resolve any complaints.

One of the biggest risks I see with clients is when they ignore consumer complaints filed with the BBB. My philosophy is to always keep a pulse on your customers. Their likes, dislikes, and most importantly their concerns. I get that the BBB is not a government regulatory body. But one thing my clients rarely know is that complaints made to the BBB still end up in the government's Consumer Sentinel Network (Sentinel).

Basically, they can become FTC complaints at a moment's notice because they're in the same system.

The Sentinel network gathers complaints from various regulatory and non-regulatory bodies, such as the Attorney General's offices, FTC, FCC, SEC, the BBB, etc. The network basically tracks complaints against companies. A company with a lot of complaints across all their sources, rather than just one, draws more attention.

And because BBB complaints are listed in the Sentinel network, it's reckless to ignore them.

The regulatory component of BBB complaints is not the only reason you should pay attention. BBB complaints give you insight into your customers. These complaints are a good way to ensure your upfront marketing is in line with your backend fulfillment. Granted, not all BBB complaints are created equal. I've responded to my share of frivolous complaints about cold coffee at events, box meals instead of three course meals, and failure to provide services when the client never once logged into the software. However, most are usually very insightful.

Of course, while a single BBB complaint doesn't automatically mean you'll get investigated by the FTC, it's one of the most common metrics you need to monitor. Having said that, a great BBB record, although very helpful and highly recommended, is not any kind of insurance against being investigated, as Anik experienced with his case.

American Association of Retired Persons

In my experience, I have found the elderly are a very vocal and protected group. In some cases, rightfully so. A few weeks before my father died in 2021, he received a call from a company telling him that if he had missed a payment for his electricity, and if he didn't immediately pay, they were going to shut off the power. Panicking, he gave the caller his credit card. Well, my father had been diagnosed with Cystic Fibrosis only the spring before, and was using an oxygen tank to supplement his breathing. Losing power would have seriously affected his ability to breathe. He got rightfully scared.

Immediately after hanging up, my dad called me and told me what had happened. In a nanosecond, I called his bank and had the card frozen. In this situation, I was more angry than I would normally be because someone had taken advantage of my helpless father. Of course, I filed a complaint with every agency known to man. But I also reverse-searched the phone number and went to war.

That's the problem with messing with the elderly; you give their family added incentive to get loud. And because of the inability of many elderly people to protect themselves, the government has put several elements in place to give them extra protection.

The elderly are also very well organized and legally represented thanks to the AARP, which advocates for those 65 and older. So, as a demographic, the AARP has the most vocal complainers and also many regulators with wide open ears to listen.

In the spirit of protecting consumers, including the most vulnerable consumers, it's no surprise that the AARP and the FTC work closely together. It's simple. If you're targeting the elderly, if you're targeting the disabled, if you're targeting those who are more susceptible and at greater risk, you're playing with fire.

Even if you are not specifically targeting this age group, but you have a great customer potential coming to you from this age group, always be extra careful. Also, remember that you can't turn them away just because of their age. That's discrimination. But I always recommend that my clients keep an extra eye on their older customers and be prepared to have a far more forgiving refund policy for them.

The AARP, the BBB, and the states all work together with the FTC and the FCC to protect consumers. If you want to avoid scrutiny by these agencies, then you must understand the rules of engagement and follow them. There is no better defense than following the law. Unfortunately, marketers are more concerned with making their first dollar than making sure that they are doing it legally. Don't let that be you.

Chapter 3:
Key Industries Tracked

Greg Christiansen

So, who does the FTC track? We already know their roots are in Mergers & Acquisitions, fraudulent advertising, privacy, and data protection. But there's a ton of other things they monitor. Everything from auto sales to healthcare comes under their jurisdiction. Let's dive into who and what the FTC is monitoring:

- Business Opportunity
    - Franchise Businesses
    - Multi-Level Marketing
    - Business Opportunity Information
- Supplements
- Health & Weight Loss
- Real Estate Investing Education
- Financial Investing Education
- Cryptocurrency
- Recurring Businesses
- Debt Reduction
- Credit Repair
- Car Dealerships
- Clothing & Textiles

This is just the tip of the iceberg. There are many more that we don't have time to get into here. But since they are all slightly unique, let's take a look at what specifically the FTC focuses on for each, along with some case examples.

Business Opportunities
In the late 1970s, several states began establishing Business Opportunity Disclosure (BODA) laws or Seller Assisted Marketing Plans Acts (SAMP). These laws were specifically created to regulate businesses, such as franchises and "make money" programs sold on infomercials.

Overtime Business Opportunities expanded to other fields. The invention of the internet created a wild west of new marketing territory. In the early 2000s, the FTC and several states started using these same 1970s laws to govern education about making money that was being sold online.

Now, only about 23 states have BODAs or SAMPs, so it's not relevant in every state. But the FTC also has similar business opportunity provisions that it enforces nationwide, so understanding these laws is still very important.

For example, the California SAMP act requires all "SAMPS" to offer a three-day right of rescission (right to cancel). Companies who fail to offer this right are not only liable to California, but also liable to private lawsuits or even a class action.

The FTC is very active in business opportunity cases.

A perfect example of this is a case against a company called "The Google Treasure Chest" or "Google Money Tree" (they went by a lot of names). In 2009, the FTC brought a case and filed a lawsuit and got a full asset freeze against the parent company for misleading consumers about starting online businesses.

These offers were doing several things wrong.

First, the company's entry-level product was a monthly subscription program that gave the customer access to information that taught them how to make money online. So, they're starting in an already highly regulated industry.

Second, Infusion failed to clearly disclose the price of the monthly subscription and the terms for canceling the subscription.

Third, the company used blatantly deceptive practices. Infusion used random online images of individuals and claimed that they were clients, then displayed fake checks and fake results.

Fourth, to make it worse, they "trapped" people by "luring" them into free or very cheap offers, without properly disclosing the buffet of subscriptions in the backend. The case focused on the many subscription services a customer would automatically get subscribed to, all for varying costs. It was a mess. I personally witnessed the collapse of the business and the personal results of the lawsuit.

The eventual settlement was for $29.5 million.

Over the years both the FTC and state regulatory bodies have expanded the scope of business opportunity laws to include many money-making informational offerings, including but not limited to:

- Real estate education
- Amazon and Walmart businesses
- Crytpo currency offerings
- Lending practices

In addition to business opportunity statutes, there are other regulatory guidelines that marketers should be aware of, such as:

1. **Franchises.** Every franchise that does business in the United States is regulated by the FTC and specific state laws. Most of these laws require the franchise company to provide detailed disclosures to all those thinking of starting that franchise.

   These disclosures include the potential risks of engaging in the franchise, as well as the substantiated and typical historical rates of returns. Failing to provide these disclosures usually means massive fines or even losing the ability to be a franchisor.

2. **Multi-Level Marketing.** We have all been prospected at one time or another by a family member or friend with promises of "being our own boss and getting residual income from an entire organization under us." This opportunity usually entails selling lotions, potions, information, kitchenware or even financial services. MLMs have been around for a long time.

   Companies like Herbalife, Young Living, Primerica, Amway, and thousands more promise to help you make money by selling the "top of the line" product in a niche. But you don't just sell the product; you recruit a team under you and get to make residuals on their sales too (and so on and so on). While there are self-regulatory bodies over MLMs, such as the Direct Sellers Association (DSA), most of the regulatory actions come by way of the FTC.

   Over the past several years, there have been massive settlements in the MLM world for earnings claims and other similar violations. Herbalife settled for $200 million and Advocare settled for $100 million, both for similar violations.

3. **Business Opportunity Education.** If you teach others how to build an online business through affiliate marketing, selling courses, Amazon, eCommerce, or any other way, you're definitely in their wheelhouse. There have been countless cases against business opportunity education companies. The main complaint? Unsubstantiated claims that are not typical results. Misuse of testimonials that are not typical and high-pressure sales techniques used on the phone (telesales).

There is definitely a recurring trend in almost all cases that the FTC goes after in this information and education industry. We'll get into that more later in this book.

Supplements

A supplement is anything that is not yet FDA approved but is taken to make you healthier.

Supplements have become easier and easier to launch. The competition for them is getting stiff, so of course, it's no surprise that the claims being made to sell them are getting crazier and crazier.

In the 1800s, traveling salesmen sold supplements, lotions, and potions we now commonly refer to as "snake oil" that could "cure" any ailment or disease. Of course, these remedies didn't actually do anything. It was all a big scam. These salesmen were known for saying whatever they had to to close a deal. That's where the term "snake oil salesman" comes from. Its roots go back to the early days of "supplements." I'm not a critic of supplements. I'm sure that they have their place and work for many individuals. I'm simply using this as an example to show the skepticism that exists, not only in the world of supplements, but in the world of marketing.

Oftentimes, marketers will embellish the underlying product and service they're offering, creating an "impression" of a certain result or outcome. The problem is that the marketer or company knows there is no way to guarantee that result or outcome, but creates the impression anyway. This is the heart of the problem the FTC has with most modern marketing. Like the snake oil salesmen of the past, companies are more concerned with the bottom line than they are with actually presenting their services in a manner that aligns with what they are selling.

Since 1998, the FTC has been involved in more than 200 cases against supplement brands. A more recent example comes from 2017, when the FTC charged NourishLife for claiming that their products could treat or prevent Alzheimers.

The company also said that their supplements were clinically proven to improve brain function and memory, and that they were endorsed by medical doctors. The FTC claimed that none of those things were true. There was no proof of clinical trials, and they couldn't find a substantial enough sample of medical doctor endorsements either. Again, the recurring theme for the FTC lies in "truthful advertising," or what they call "misleading advertising."

However, when it comes to supplements, there is added risk, because you are not only concerned about the representations violating Section 5 of the FTC Act, but you also need to ensure the marketing does not go against FDA guidelines. FDA guidelines are there because many of these supplements are not regulated. Companies have not gone through the rigors of scientific testing and evaluation that is required for the promotion of a "drug." Because of this lower standard, supplement companies cannot expressly state or create the impression that its supplements can help "prevent, cure, or treat" any type of sickness or disease.

Health Offers

Outside of supplements, you have a lot of education being sold around healthier living, weight loss, and now, biohacking. You don't have to sell supplements to fall into trouble for making claims. Many companies have faced issues for either explicitly saying or implying that they can cure an illness.

Let's take Agora Financial for example. This is a very large company in the information marketing world. It's not only a very successful company, but one that most all information marketers use as a model to follow. One of their many divisions is in the health space, which sold "The Doctor's Guide to Reversing Diabetes in 28 Days." The FTC alleged that there was no research, proof, or record of the information in the guide having a "typical result" of curing diabetes.

This got the FTC knocking on their door, eventually settling for over $2 million.

Real Estate Investing Education

Decades ago, it became common to go to a hotel for a "free" event to learn how to become rich using real estate investing. You would walk in for free and walk out having bought a $50,000 package in the snap of a finger.

Or you would watch an infomercial for that "golden book" that would show you the way to passive real estate profits. In 2011, the FTC brought action against Russell Dalbey for a program called "Winning in the Cash Flow Business." Dalby ran a 30-minute infomercial where he sold an initial product that would end up costing the customer between $40 and $120. But that was just the beginning.

After that, the customer would get hammered with upsell after upsell. And according to the FTC, there was never proof of overwhelming success from the training. This was the case that started the FTC crusade against the real estate training industry. Over the years, there have been actions against *Russ Whitney, Sr., Zurrix, Nudge,* and many other real estate training companies.

And as we speak, we are aware of other real estate education companies under investigation. This is definitely a niche of key interest to the regulators.

Financial Investing Education
The FTC has also expanded its reach into companies giving investment training, often teaming up with the SEC. The FTC and SEC have brought actions against investment "training" companies for decades.

Seminars, online training, webinars, virtual events—there is no shortage of companies teaching you how to do things such as day trade, trade options, or trade commodities. While the SEC and FINRA is the main governing body of the "investment advice" side of it, it is the FTC who governs the marketing and advertising side of it.

In 2020, the FTC brought two cases against financial training companies, The Online Trading Academy (OTA) and RagingBull.com, LLC., which have become staples in the discussion on compliance. The FTC alleged that OTA specifically targeted "retirement age" individuals to offer stock trading training to help them see huge returns in their retirement plans. OTA was accused of using "false or unsubstantiated earnings claims." In the end, the settlement cost the company, and some of the key individuals involved, nearly $10 million.

Maryland-based RagingBull provides stock trading training. The company was scaling fast on paid traffic and was accused of the same thing as OTA, "False or Unsubstantiated Earnings Claims." The FTC had other violations against RagingBull, but the earnings claims were their main focus in the beginning. This investigation ended up costing RagingBull a settlement of $2.4 million.

There have since been countless other settlements in the financial education industry, making it another active niche for regulators.

Cryptocurrency

With the surge of interest in cryptocurrencies, it's no surprise that many companies have popped up selling education or even directly selling crypto and crypto hardware. There's now a booming multibillion dollar industry in this space. The only difference is that people are being told they will get certain results from crypto (versus stock or business). Otherwise, the customer claims are the same. And if the claims are the same, the FTC will step in.

In 2016, the FTC halted the operations of Bitcoin Funding Team and My7Network for allegedly deceiving consumers with false income claims. According to the complaint, the companies advertised that users could "earn an unlimited amount of money" by using their crypto referral program. The FTC found that, in fact, very few participants earned substantial incomes, while the vast majority lost money. The regulator stated that unsupported returns were being used to market the scheme. In the end, there was an "ability to pay" settlement of over $450,000.

As cryptocurrencies remain highly speculative assets, regulators like the FTC and SEC are busy. I expect to see a lot more activity in this space, as crypto has been picking up even more steam in recent years.

If you sell crypto, are a crypto exchange, sell any education about crypto, or even sell crypto hardware, you're officially in a very regulated space.

Recurring Businesses

In November, 2022, the FTC settled with Vonage for almost $100 million because they accused Vonage of making it too difficult to cancel a subscription. Apple, AT&T, Amazon, XM Sirius, Match.com, and many other major players have been sued by the FTC over their recurring billing.

Countless smaller companies have also been hit. The FTC is not at all concerned with company size, revenue, or popularity. They will sue any company or individual that they believe is violating the law. So, if you sell subscriptions to training programs, SaaS, or any online retail, you need to specifically focus on the ROSCA rules, something we dive deeper into later in this book.

Debt Reduction

As consumer debt rises in this country at an alarming rate, numerous companies keep emerging every year offering inflated debt relief services. Many of these companies are overpromising the amount of debt reduction that is possible, while underdelivering on the actual results. Of course, this has captured the attention of the FTC and many other regulators (including state regulators).

Going back as far as 2006, the FTC settled with AmeriDebt in a case that eventually returned over $13 million to consumers. AmeriDebt was alleged to be masquerading as a non-profit, yet charged obscene fees to help consumers with debt relief. The FTC claimed they did not properly deliver on their promise, yet made millions from those fees.

Similarly, in 2023, the FTC stopped a company called Express Enrollment for allegedly charging $8 million in junk fees for "student debt relief" services that never happened. The case led to a $7.4 million settlement.

These are just a couple of examples in debt relief, which is a very active space for the FTC, so much so that they're beginning to focus even more on it. In 2022, there were three settlements with debt relief companies. In 2023, there were ten. It's only going in one direction.

Mergers & Acquisitions
The FTC is an active governing body regardless of what industry you're in. It should come as no surprise that they step in to block mergers if they think the resulting company will be too big. Remember, blocking monopolies was the original focus of the FTC.

One example of a merger that the FTC is currently fighting (at the time of writing this book) is between Microsoft and Activision Blizzard, Inc. Activision is a gaming company that created Call of Duty, World of Warcraft, and Candy Crush, among other very popular games.

The FTC claimed that if Activision is to merge with Microsoft, it will eliminate competition for Microsoft's Xbox. So far, the FTC has lost their case, but they're not giving up and are currently appealing.

In another example, Staples and Office Depot tried to merge twice, once in 1997 and once in 2016, and in both cases, the FTC has intervened and stopped it.

Another industry the FTC has recently been active in is Pharmaceuticals, from stopping a merger between Pfizer and Allergan in 2016 to recently suing a Pharma broker (for artificially raising drug prices to benefit mergers). In fact, there were many cases in 2022 and 2023 of pharmaceutical mergers being stopped to help regulate the price of medications.

Credit Repair

With consumer credit being vital for many major purchases, companies advertising credit repair services have exploded lately. However, many of these companies flat out fail to improve credit scores, yet continue to advertise that they have success at doing so. As a result, the FTC has begun closely monitoring this industry.

In 2022, the FTC got a restraining order on a company called "The Credit Game." They were accused of using deceptive marketing, such as fake identity theft reports. They were also accused of selling services that cost hundreds to thousands of dollars with little to no results in actually helping repair the consumers' credit score.

Similarly, in 2022, the FTC got a restraining order against Turbo Solutions, Inc. and its founders for pretty much the same. They were charging hundreds of dollars for services that were non-existent and had no track record of success.

Considering that most credit repair offers are sold to those who are already in financial distress, and perhaps desperate, the regulators take a very keen interest in this space. Any time you find a less fortunate consumer, you will find increased regulator activity.

Hidden Fees

One of the most recent additions to the FTC's arsenal of weapons is its policies about hidden fees. Have you ever checked into a resort and seen the barrage of fees, such as a "resort fee"? Ever wondered what that is exactly? After all, you're paying for a room that exists inside the resort. Is that not the only "fee" that matters?

Imagine filling your tank with gas, and the station adding a "filling station" fee. Your reaction to this is shared by the FTC; they don't like it. And the cases against what they call "hidden fees" have begun.

Key Industries Tracked

Here are examples of what they consider hidden (or junk) fees:

- Booking fees
- Resort fees
- Service charges at restaurants
- Processing fee
- Application fee
- Cancellation fee
- Overdraft fee
- Seat selection fee
- Fuel surcharge fee

Many everyday businesses are making big money by charging these unnecessary fees, which are never properly disclosed. The FTC has thoroughly warned companies that their time for charging these types of fees is rapidly coming to an end.

One of the most recent cases related to hidden fees is against car dealerships. Recently, the FTC brought a case against Chase/Manchester City Nissan out of Connecticut for charging hidden fees (the case is currently paused). The FTC cited the dealership for offering a "certified" used car fee, even when Nissan corporate expressly prohibits dealerships from doing this.

The FTC claimed that the dealership, in addition to deceiving consumers, regularly charged "junk fees" for certification, add-on products, and government charges without the consumers' consent."

Clothing and Textiles

I wanted to throw a unique example in here for you, something to show you the variety of the things that the FTC is looking for. In the clothing industry, the FTC helps manufacturers label products made of certain types of material, including cashmere, cotton, down, feather, fur, wool, and rayon, which is made from bamboo. If a label says "100% cotton," that's a claim that is fair game to be reviewed.

A specific claim in the clothing industry that has come under their attention is the claim of "Made in the USA." In many cases, making this claim can help a product sell better, and even sell for a higher amount. In May 2023, the FTC settled a suit against "Lions Not Sheep" for allegedly replacing "Made in China" tags with "Made in the USA" tags.

I personally know the founder of this company, and I know that most of the product line was, in fact, made in the United States. However, I still advised the founder to settle. The problem in these situations is that the cost to litigate a case like this is very expensive. It would have cost him far more than a quick settlement with the FTC. He ended up settling for $176,000 in fines.

In another example, the FTC brought a case against Williams-Sonoma for wrongfully claiming certain products were made in the USA, when they were wholly imported. Williams-Sonoma settled for $1 million.

If you learn anything from this chapter, it is that the FTC and regulatory agencies have a large reach over various types of businesses and industries. The key is truthfulness in advertising. Any products or services directed at consumers falls under the all-encompassing power of the FTC.

Chapter 4:
The Three Most Common Federal Laws the FTC Uses

Greg Christiansen

Even though the FTC has its fingers in a lot of areas of regulation, my primary focus is advertising and marketing claims. The biggest problem with advertising agencies and marketing companies is that they don't understand the rules. I would even go as far as to say that some of the largest companies in the riskiest industries frankly just don't care about compliance. I see it all the time.

- "I don't want to know the rules because I could never convert."
- "Compliance attorneys don't ever help you; they only hurt you."
- "I'll just keep on doing what I'm doing and will deal with the feds if something happens."

I'm not arguing that advice from every counsel is helpful, but advice from the right counsel is vital.

One of my favorite movies growing up was the Untouchables with Sean Conery and Kevin Costner. There is a scene where a thug shows up at Sean Conery's apartment with a knife, and Conery tells him, "You never bring a knife to a gunfight." It's one of the greatest lines in cinema.

Unfortunately for Conery's character, he walks right into a trap and loses his life. You don't want to walk into a similar (albeit less dramatic) trap.

Don't Say That

You don't want to be out there saying things incorrectly and red flagging your business with the regulators, when all along you can get similar results without breaking the rules.

It is naive and incredibly reckless to think that you will just deal with it when it happens. Ask Anik—he would have done anything to avoid the pain he went through.

Before we get into the weeds, let's break down the key elements of the FTC Act, which is the one that is most referred to in advertising regulation. These sections are the repeated primary focus of the FTC:

- Section 5
- Section 13(b)
- Section 19

I don't want to imply that these are the only sections of the FTC Act you need to be in compliance with. I'm saying these are the primary players. If you understand and comply with these, then you can rest assured that your marketing meets the federal guidelines.

Section 5

Section 5 is at the top of the FTC compliance organizational chart. All regulatory actions brought by the FTC are done under the authority of Section 5. Section 5 is a prohibition against "Unfair and Deceptive Acts or Practices." Under section 5, acts or practices are "unfair" if the advertisement:

- Causes or is likely to cause substantial injury to consumers
- Causes injury that cannot be reasonably avoided
- Causes damage to the consumer that is greater than any benefits received

Practices and acts are "deceptive" when:

- A representation (or omission) is likely to mislead the consumer
- A consumer's interpretation of the representation (or omission) is reasonable
- The misrepresentation is material

The laws, as written, can be very hard to understand. They can also sound vague. Let's simplify everything by using an exaggerated example to help make sense of it.

Let's say you have an advertisement selling a Porsche 911. The advertisement is specific. It shows pictures and videos of a beautiful 911. The marketing talks about how much the driver loves the feel of driving a 911 and about all the exciting features of the Porsche 911.

Clearly what is being sold is a Porsche 911.

However, when you go to the dealer to see the car, the company flips the script and offers you a "comparable" Volkswagen Beetle. Wait, what happened to the Porsche? The reviews you read and ads you saw were about a Porsche. You want the Porsche, yet you're getting a Bug.

Same company. Different product.

I know this is an obvious and extreme example, but this is the kind of marketing I'm seeing in the Information Industry all the time. In the eyes of a regulator, the Porsche example is just as obvious and bad as the example below...

> *"Look at Kim. She's a stay at home mom who makes $9,500.00 a month, all while working part-time, selling*

> products on Amazon. Purchase our coaching, and we'll help put you in the same position as Kim! Within months, you can quit your job and live the lifestyle you've always dreamed of."

That's the Porsche.

Now, what they leave out of the marketing is the truth that most customers actually experience. They leave out the fact that most of the people who purchase the $10,000.00 course get frustrated, invest and lose even more money, get lost in challenge after challenge, and don't stick around long enough to see results. Basically, the true "average customer" is not Kim, the Porsche, it's someone who achieves a very different "result."

That's the Volkswagen Beetle.

I've heard all of the justifications:

- My customers are lazy.
- They quit too soon.
- They didn't do all of the work we told them to do.
- They didn't take it seriously.
- They barely tried.
- They're not smart enough to do this.

My response is always the same.

If you go back to the impression (the FTC calls it the "Net Impression") you're giving your customers through your marketing, what would a "reasonable" person believe? What would they think you are offering?

Would they think...

A) I'm going to be able to quickly and easily make some money on Amazon, quit my job, and pay off all this debt I have. Then I can take luxurious vacations and buy ferraris.

Or

B) They're here to give me systems, help, and support to develop a new skill. I'm going to learn how to sell products on Amazon, and then it's up to me to figure it out. This business may or may not work for me.

Chances are, most marketing you review is closer to giving the net impression in A, rather than B.

Despite this, I have many clients that argue with me, "But Greg, it works if they just do it!"

My question is always, "It works for who?"

You can't pick out the select few of your customers who showed the determination, willpower, and coachability to actually finish your program, implement it, and succeed. Unless that is the typical average person, you can't cherry pick their stories and base your marketing on it.

And that, in a nutshell, is Section 5. Section 5 is all about truthful marketing practices and the impressions being created. The goal is to make sure the promises you give in your marketing and advertising are truthful and also in alignment with the product the customer actually gets.

Remember, you have no control over the outcome someone has by taking your product. Hence, you cannot base your marketing on it.

You can say a Porsche is fast, that is under your control and it's proven. However you can't say "Buy this Porsche and win the next Daytona race." You have no control over the outcome.

So, for example, if you're teaching people how to invest in the stock market.

Bad: "We'll show you how to have an 86% win rate and make 36% a month. Start making $1,000 a day within the first year." You have no control over or ability to create this. And, if you truly do, make sure you have "typical results" studies and can back it up.

Or else...

Good: "Our product can help you learn how to invest in the market. We teach you the foundations and the specific strategies used by our best trading coaches. We put you in a much better position to win through our advice, coaching, community, and more. This is for those who want to truly learn how to invest, not for those just looking to make some fast money, because you won't. So, if you're looking to finally learn how to invest, let us help you."

It may not be as sexy, but trust me, it works and it brings you far better customers. This is precisely how the biggest companies market. The "results claim" is typically only seen by direct marketing companies, who all end up building horrible customer bases. So, compliance with Section 5 actually helps you build a stronger business.

Section 13(b)

Section 13(b) gives the FTC specific powers in the case of Section 5 violations. It allows the FTC to use its authority to put an immediate stop to a business they believe is using unfair and deceptive advertising. Basically, it adds additional legal authority on top of Section 5.

Section 13(b) allows the FTC to quickly address questionable products, services, and claims that could be harming consumers. Section 13(b) also allows the FTC to go further and ask a federal court to issue an immediate injunction against a company and shut them down very quickly.

An injunction is a court order demanding the company stop what they're doing right away, while the investigation and litigation begins. Instead of following the typical extensive legal process, the FTC can accelerate cases under 13(b) in what they deem urgent situations.

For example, let's say a company is selling an unverified COVID treatment. The FTC could shut it down very quickly using 13(b). It's obvious how this could hurt consumers, if the treatment is unproven and potentially not safe. In this case, the FTC doesn't need to go through a long legal process to stop the company from selling the product, which may be required under Section 5. It can simply petition a court with proof and get a judge to sign an order, shutting the company down immediately.

Imagine a business opportunity that is generating millions a year selling extreme claims. If they have zero documentation, proof, or substantiation, and they're taking thousands of dollars from consumers, leaving them running during an investigation could harm many more people. Hence, the FTC can move under 13(b) and get the entire operation shutdown fast.

Section 13(b) was the FTC's primary tool of enforcement until 2021. For more than 40 years, the FTC relied on 13(b) to not only stop companies, but to freeze their assets and fine them to the maximum possible amount. For 40 years, federal judges throughout the United States allowed the FTC to obtain full asset freezes and take millions of dollars of money as restitution.

In April 2021, the Supreme Court heard arguments against the FTC and ultimately reached a pivotal decision. The Supreme Court ruled that, while Section 13(b) allows the FTC to immediately stop businesses from engaging in deceptive practices, it does not include language that gives the FTC authority to charge fines, get restitution, or collect any monetary relief.

The FTC lost the case against the Supreme Court. After losing the ability to collect money or freeze assets from companies under investigation, the FTC has made a change in how they approach their cases. They have now shifted their focus to Section 19. This section focuses even more specifically on telesales and "one-to-one" sales of any kind.

Section 19

Section 19 empowers the FTC to issue very targeted rules for the telemarketing industry. This includes all modes of "one-to-one selling." Telephone, Zoom, the backroom of an event—anything where a sales representative is having a personal conversation is governed under Section 19.

For example, under Section 19, the FTC created the "Telemarketing Sales Rule (TSR)," which regulates false or misleading statements being made to get a sale. This includes, but is not limited to, falsely representing the price, potential returns, product effectiveness, earnings potential, or any other representations that push a consumer into an unfair sale.

Let's talk about warranties. If a salesperson is pitching extended warranties for your car, but is exaggerating the potential future repair costs or strategically leaving out things that are already covered, this would be a section 19 violation. Or if an investment fund is on the phone and heavily exaggerating their past performance and your future earnings, yet again, this is a violation.

Basically, Section 19 is about truthful and fair advertising practices in one-on-one situations. It expands further upon Section 5 through its specificity by allowing the FTC to seek consumer redress (fines). Section 19 also differs from Section 13(b) in that, unlike 13(b), 19 allows the FTC to freeze assets, levy fines, collect damages, and much more. It then comes as no surprise that the FTC is currently focusing most of their activity and investigations under Section 19.

Now that we understand the agencies and the laws, let's move on to talk about investigations, specifically the investigation Anik went through. He's going to tell his story of what it felt like under the microscope, and why you never want to experience any of it. Ever.

If you think you're immune, think again. Anik never thought it would happen to him. He had a great record and ran a great company. However, as it turned out, the rules are the rules and they were enough to get him into hot water.

Part 2:
The Cost of Not Complying

Chapter 5:
"This Won't Happen to Me"

Anik Singal

To be honest, I never saw it coming. I thought that the FTC only went after the heathens and swindlers, people who are outright scamming and disappearing. I had a physical training center, impeccable customer service records, no lawsuits, no merchant account issues, and overall very happy customers. This wasn't by chance. We ran an amazing company and spent millions to make sure our customers were taken care of.

As it turns out, all that was great and helpful, but it wasn't enough. I've talked to a lot of people, and still do to this day, who just don't take the FTC seriously. They consistently seem to feel they are safe from any lawsuit. Why? Well, let's go over the five most common reasons I hear.

Common Myths

Unfortunately, I see this all the time. When companies get hit by the FTC or State regulatory bodies, most who see the case think, "This won't happen to me. I'm different." All too often, however, it does happen, and it's happening more and more frequently.

The common myths:

1. We're too small for the FTC to care.
2. We have great customer service, so we're good.
3. We don't have a volume of customer complaints.
4. We're honest and deliver good value.
5. We're not based in the United States.

Don't Say That

Let's see some real-world data and case examples to debunk each of these.

We're too small for the FTC to care
Ever since my experience with the FTC began in 2021, I've been hearing the same thing over and over from business owners.

"I'm too small to get sued by the FTC."

Everytime I hear it, I shake my head. That mentality is dangerous.

The FTC and other regulatory bodies have repeatedly made one thing crystal clear. No one is too small to be investigated or sued. There is no "minimum threshold" required to be targeted. The law is the law, and it applies to everyone regardless of your size. The Amazons and Facebooks of the world may get the big headlines, but every single month, small companies around the world end up being investigated.

Because I am sick of hearing this misstatement, I did some research. This is what I found:

- A1 Docprep had only 136 eligible customers and was fined $232,755.
- CD Capital Investments had only 243 eligible customers and was fined $132,072.
- Manhattan Beach Venture had only 2,889 eligible customers and was fined $292,200.
- Campbell Capital had only 603 eligible customers and was fined $30,000.
- Vision Solution Marketing had only 1,177 customers and was fined $1.67 million (a case Greg represented).

Greg himself talks about clients he's represented, one of whom settled for $15,000 and another one who settled by giving the FTC just his watch. So, no, you are never too small to get investigated.

Do the big companies get all the big headlines? Of course.

Are small companies almost bankrupted by the burden of being investigated regularly? The answer is a loud yes.

Never let the fact that "you're a small company" prevent you from becoming compliant. Plus, small companies want to become big one day, and the habits you set up today will only magnify as you grow.

You want the right foundation, one that is following the law.

We have great customer service
This was me.

I truly bragged about our customer service, and I believed it alone would protect me. We had three support teams worldwide, strategically placed so we could run 24/7 support. Nights. Weekends. Holidays. We had an average response time of 36 minutes. Yes, this was even after doing over 60,000 transactions in a three year window. Not just that, but we had below a 5% refund rate. Our chargeback rate was below .7%, which is less than half of the Industry standard.

Our BBB rating was an A. We had no legal issues. We had no major complaints. Yet, that was simply not enough. As impressive as that feat was, it didn't stop us from being investigated on the letter of the law.

Great customer service is vital.
I highly encourage you to have it. Heck, I encourage you to have a department even better than mine. However, don't live in the myth that

happy customers and serviced customers will protect you from regulatory eyes. It won't.

We don't have a volume of customer complaints

We always put our customers first. In addition to the excellent customer support, we offered a lot of perks and bonuses to our students. And, when and if there was an upset customer, we put priority on them with one-on-one support.

Bottom line, all our practices meant that we had very few customer complaints. We had no legal cases. No Attorney General cases. No issues at all from what I could see.

But an absence of customer complaints isn't what we think it is in the eyes of the FTC and other regulators. They see complaints and refund requests as just the tip of the iceberg. They believe that most unsatisfied customers just don't say anything. They think if you have even a few complaints, it means that you likely have hundreds of upset consumers. Hence, the argument of "we don't have many complaints" is going to fall on deaf ears.

Complaints do play a vital role in their decisions. However, it's not in your favor. High complaints means you're almost definitely going to get investigated. However, low complaints doesn't mean you won't.

There are many cases in which the regulators have gone after companies that had great customer records. It all comes back to the law. The ads. The sales material. The claims. That is what carries the most weight.

We are honest and deliver good value

Whenever I thought about the FTC, I used very simple thinking. I figured they're there to protect consumers from outright scams. They're there to protect people from getting robbed. They go after those who are hurting people.

This gave me a great feeling of protection because I didn't see myself doing any of those things. My customers love me. I'm in the open and teaching all day long. I provide amazing value and I take care of my customers, not hurt them.

In the end, the truth is that "good value" is a subjective argument, and even then, an irrelevant one. It all comes down to what you're saying, what you're claiming, and whether you can substantiate it in their eyes. Again, the rules are the rules regardless of the level of service you're providing.

Most of us love Amazon. We use it daily in our lives. We thank Amazon for being so fast and trustworthy, yet, as we write this book, Amazon is being sued by the FTC.

We're not based in the United States
First, if you're a U.S. citizen, it doesn't matter where you base your company. Remember, the FTC and other regulators have jurisdiction over you personally and your company. So, if your company is out of the country, they will simply go after you.

Now, what if you're not a U.S. citizen and your company is not inside the U.S.? Well, are you selling inside the U.S.? If you're selling to U.S. consumers, then the laws still pertain to you. The FTC has had many cases where they partner with your local country authorities and still come for you.

One example is the MOBE (My Online Business Empire) case, which was settled in 2022. MOBE was a Canadian company, and the owner was not a U.S. Citizen. They had companies based all over the world. Not only did they go after him, but they actually confiscated properties that were outside the United States as part of a massive settlement. In this case (as with many others), the company and the main founder were not American. However, the fact that they did business in the U.S. was enough.

So, unfortunately, your fancy Cayman Island trust that holds Swiss companies is not going to protect you from the advertising law.

To further hit home the fact that it definitely can happen to you, in the next chapter, I'm going to share some data that proves you're probably not as compliant as you thought.

Chapter 6:
How FTC Enforcement Has Changed

Greg Christiansen

Obviously, the FTC has changed over the years. It's been more than a century since they began, and technology alone prompted a lot of the changes. But in 2021, something specific happened that led to one of the biggest changes they've ever made. It's important you understand this particular change.

Post AMG Capital Management (April, 2021).

As discussed earlier, the Supreme Court reached a pivotal decision on April 22, 2021 that fundamentally changed how the FTC enforces their main rules. Before this ruling, the FTC often used Section 13(b) to freeze assets, enforce financial fines, and consumer redress.

But the Supreme Court ruled in the AMG Capital Management case that Section 13(b) does not, in fact, give the FTC the ability to ask for any kind of redress or fines. All they can do is shut down the business. No more asset freezes. No more consumer redress.

In comes a change, the "notice of penalty offenses."

Notice of Penalty Offenses

Section 5 gives the FTC the authority to impose fines per offense, provided the company has been specifically warned about their violations prior to the fines. The warnings have to be specific and quote past cases that determine the law to be final in court.

Shortly after the ruling, the FTC pivoted and decided to put hundreds of companies "on notice," using a blanket letter that was not quite specific, but in their eyes, sufficient. The warnings they sent out were called "Notice of Penalty Offenses," and they specifically spoke about the use of testimonials. The warnings were not definitive in the eyes of many companies. However, for the FTC, this would be the beginning of them applying actual fines under Section 5.

The letters warned that every infraction thereof could result in a fine of as much as $43,792 per offense (as of today they have raised it to $50,120). Then they decided to use that warning as a "first contact," so if they eventually sued your company, they could claim you were specifically warned but did not make changes.

The idea of this $50,120 per infraction actually being enforceable is under debate right now. It has yet to be tested in court. However, it is currently being used to investigate companies. But lawyers are now seeing a trend, the same as we did with Anik. The warning under Section 5 is indeed being followed by official investigations, if you don't make drastic changes.

Section 5 is simply being used to open the doors to the investigation. However, once the process begins, the FTC narrows in and focuses on Section 19 for actual monetary fines.

Section 13(b) & Section 19

While Section 13(b) is still a major rule and serves a strong purpose, it hasn't been getting used as much. Instead, the focus is shifting to Section 19, which is the part of the act that specifically focuses on one-to-one communications or "telesales."

As previously discussed, the Supreme Court ruling did not apply to Section 19, so the FTC is still able to freeze assets, collect monetary judgment, and more, as long as the accused company is using telesales in their business.

Here's an example of a case where the FTC was allowed to use Section 19, instead of Section 13(b), to obtain financial restitution. There was a company called Credit Bureau Center that the FTC accused of deceiving consumers by charging them without consent. The court originally ordered Credit Bureau Center to pay over $5 million to consumers under Section 13(b).

On appeal, the monetary award based on Section 13(b) was thrown out because of the Supreme Court ruling that had happened in the meantime. But the FTC had their own twist. They simply petitioned the court to change from Section 13(b) to Section 19.

The court allowed it, and the $5 million restitution was back in place. As a result, most cases now being brought by the FTC are being fought under Section 19 (as was Anik's case).

So, the biggest change for the FTC is that they are now focusing their efforts even more on companies that are doing "one-to-one" sales or using recurring revenue in their business. They're still able to enforce fines for these businesses under Section 19.

Marketer's Perspective

Anik Singal

The rules are the rules, and right now, my biggest suggestion to marketers is, if you don't need to have telesales as a part of your business, get rid of it immediately. Doing one-to-one sales right now is a liability. Even recurring revenue is tricky, but it's easier to do, as long as you're using full disclosures and following the law.

However, most businesses I know have some form of telephone, Zoom, or live event sales. If that's the case, and it's vital to your business, I recommend you get very serious about making sure every sales call is 100% compliant. Not, 95% or 97% compliant—100%.

Chapter 7:
What It Costs to Be Investigated

Anik Singal

Whenever someone asks me how much my settlement cost me, I cringe because I know what's coming next. The actual fine amount was $2.5 million, but here's why I hate telling people that.

"*Just $2.5 million? That's not bad at all for the millions you made!*"

My head almost explodes with anger at the naivety and complete lack of understanding.

The actual fine is just the tip of the iceberg. The real question should be, "What did the *investigation* cost you?" If I were to give you my opinion, the total cost was closer to $15 million, once you factor in the lawyer's fees, the settlement, the lost opportunity cost, and the impact to my business. That doesn't even cover the more than one hundred sleepless nights, the PTSD, and a forever fear of receiving certified letters or FedEx packages.

Let me explain.

I want to discuss all the costs, both monetary and non-monetary. Let's tackle them one at a time. The financial cost of being investigated can be grouped into the following categories:

- The Lawyers
- The Discovery
- The Fine (Consumer Redress)
- Loss of Business Opportunity

Each one of these is substantial. You have to figure in all of these in order to get the whole picture, not just the wire I sent to the FTC.

The Lawyers

You're going to have to hire a law firm. In my case, I hired two (I like to be thorough). I always believe in getting multiple opinions, and I would absolutely recommend the same to anyone else.

If you hire a smaller law firm, the investigation could cost you between $100,000 to $500,000. But if you opt for a larger law firm, you will be paying a minimum of $500,000, and even as high as $2 million in during the investigation, and that's just legal fees.

I'm not advocating either way. To each their own. There are benefits to having a larger firm, and there are benefits to having a smaller firm. You have to look at your own situation to see which attorney fits you. Just make sure the attorney you choose has a very specific expertise. Whichever regulating agency is investigating you, that agency should be their speciality. Period. Look at their experience, look at their bio, and look specifically for the name of the agency that is investigating you.

For me, my legal bills were approximately $700,000.

The Discovery

The discovery has two main costs to it:

1. The team members that do the document collection.
2. The forensics companies that pull the required data.

First and foremost, I had to take at least seven of my best team members and assign them full-time to collecting all the documents needed. The list from the FTC was huge. Here's a small sample (you can get a full summary at www.DontSayThat.com/cid):

- Financial records
- Customer data
- Past advertising campaigns
- All versions of every advertisement
- All past landing pages
- Copies of all customer complaints
- Every single refund request and response
- Every sales call
- All contracts ever signed
- List of all partners and anyone paid by the company
- Copies of all legal issues and settlements
- All merchant statements
- A copy of every communication within the company (Email, slack, text, etc.)
- CRM access

The list is so extensive that one person on their own could never do it. Personally, I wouldn't have even known where 90% of the information was. So, I ended up needing to assign about seven of my full-time team members for almost nine months to do nothing but collect paperwork.

And to make it worse, these were my best team members; the ones who had been with me the longest and the ones who earned the highest compensation. I would estimate that the salaries alone to cover these team members was close to $1 million.

Don't Say That

Next, in comes the forensics companies. The FTC wants to see all internal communications between all employees. I had no idea that you could even pull every Email, every Slack communication, every Skype conversation. Turns out, you can. It just has to be done by professionals, who charge an arm and a leg. I estimate having spent around $200,000 on forensics companies, consultants, and contractors to help us dig out the data that the FTC needed.

So, all in all, $1.2 million of hard cost just to collect the documents the FTC needed to investigate us.

The Fine

This one is obvious. In the end, the FTC will demand a specific number for consumer redress. They started with $14 million for me because that was the full amount that we sold on the phone. They wanted it all. I would like to say that we heavily negotiated, but that's not how it works with the Government.

You can't negotiate, but you can lean on something called "ability to pay."

In order to qualify under this clause, you need to agree to revealing all your financials, every penny, every collectible, every trust, every property, every crypto, all of it. Based on what you have that is "available relatively quickly," they will determine what you can pay at that time.

Real estate? They can ask you to sell it.

Cars? They can ask you to sell them.

Crypto? Convert it.

Stocks? Cash out.

If it's liquid, it goes into the calculation, and their goal is to take a substantial amount of that figure. I believe every case is different and the level of your infractions definitely seem to play a role in how flexible the FTC will be. In the end, they have many players they want to go after so settling is also in their favor. But don't bother thinking that you can bluff them. If they need to go to court, they absolutely will.

In the end, although I considered going to court many times, I knew that a case like mine could take years in litigation and about $3 million or more in legal fees, plus even more psychological damage. It was too much.

So, all in all, we decided to settle for $2.5 million. Not a number that I was happy about, but a number I could live with, so I could get back to my life and get back to building my business and being an Entrepreneur.

Loss of Business Opportunities

I think the loss of business opportunity is likely the highest cost that very few people even consider. At the time that we got our CID (May, 2022), we were about to break our record and have the most profitable month in the history of the company.

Not only that, but 2022 was looking like an amazing year where we would break the next level of success, and we were projecting to do $40 million at over 15% profit margin. And 2023 was looking even stronger.

Add to that the fact that we were in final talks about being acquired. I would have had my entrepreneurial dream of selling the company come true. Instead, in May 2022, I had to shut down 80% of our product lines. Being a Publishing company, we were reliant on products that were under different brands and experts. The minute I got the CID, I would not risk any of them still being promoted.

So, within 48 hours, I made the impossible decision to shut down 80% of a $40 million-a-year company, which also resulted in me having to lay off almost 80% of our team. The effect of this was crippling. I had invested 20 years perfecting the incredibly difficult business model of publishing and hiring the absolute best people to build it.

The very month that we had finally figured it out. The very year where we would be acquired. The very moment my team was perfect and final, I ended up having to completely shut it down.

So, what was my monetary "lost opportunity" cost? I could say it was as low as $10 million, or even as high as $50 million. The real number is somewhere in between.

Why Settle & Not Just Go To Court?

Simple. It's damn expensive, and it's mental torture. There were many times that I got frustrated with the process and wanted to go to trial. I wanted to prove that things about me were being exaggerated. However, the matter came down to the following:

1. It would cost an estimated $3 million to $5 million to properly defend myself.
2. There would be countless depositions for me, my team, and my customers.
3. Discovery would begin again.
4. I wouldn't be able to move forward to build something else.
5. As a father of two young girls, I would always have this monkey on my back, distracting me from being the best father I can be.

Greg gave me the perfect example of a case he was representing at the time that was in trial. There were seven attorneys from the defense side, all sitting in the same court room at the same time, and this was projected to go on for 5 weeks. I did the math. The defendant could end up spending as much as $70,000 a day for their defense, and that was just during the trial. It didn't include the hundreds of hours of preparation that led up to the trial.

The burden, the cost, the psychological impact—for me, in the end, it just wasn't worth it. Not to mention the risk. In the end, a Judge or Jury may just agree with the FTC, and the fine levied on me could be far greater than the settlement cost. All in all, the smart decision, the one lacking emotion, was to settle, not as an admission of guilt, but as a way to get my life back and be allowed to move forward.

And even though I estimate that the total cost to me was $15 million or more, I stand by my decision. I settled, and I got to move on.

Lawyer's Perspective

Greg Christiansen

I'm not afraid of a fight. If there is no way to negotiate, and there is no reason on the other side, then you are forced to litigate the issues. But litigation is generally the least effective way to resolve a dispute. When there is an opportunity to negotiate a settlement, you should do it, especially when fighting with government-backed agencies. Furthermore, the cost of litigation extends past the financial burden; the mental toll it takes is tremendous. I've seen clients fall into depression, have major anxiety, and end up needing medication. Some have even died from the stress or taken their own life. The entire process is very grueling.

If nothing else, going to trial is a guaranteed way to lose years of your life.

No matter what happens, getting a Civil Investigative Demand (CID), or being sued by the government, is always going to be an expensive ordeal.

Don't Say That

You should always make sure you have a great attorney, but at the same time, stay vigilant of who is on each and every call. The larger the firm, the more attorneys on the call, the more that call is costing you. Keep a close eye on your legal bills, and communicate with your attorney, because there are ways to save money.

In short, it's going to be expensive no matter what. But with a CID, you can manage your costs and have far more control than when it goes to trial. So, unless you have a very unique situation, it's usually best to settle.

Chapter 8:
The Non-Monetary Cost of Being Investigated

Anik Singal

Not only is the price tag on an FTC investigation sky high, but there are other, non-monetary consequences that are far worse:

- Sleepless nights
- Nose-diving health
- Reputation damage
- Potential forever bans
- Additional lawsuits
- Loss of employees
- Loss of business

The list goes on…

In my case, I would say the psychological side of the investigation is what I will remember more than anything else. I genuinely have PTSD when it comes to certified letters or FedEx packages. The thought of a lawsuit of any kind now immediately makes me flush. From gaining weight to having multiple flare-ups of my health condition to nearly falling into depression—these are the sides of a government investigation that no one talks about.

But I will.

The crazy thing is that during the investigation, you're working day and night to cooperate, which means digging up thousands and thousands of documents. You're also fighting hard to survive and save your business. However, on the FTC side, it's just business as usual. They have many cases, and when you turn over thousands of documents, they rightfully need many hours, days, weeks, and even months to review them.

There would be times in the investigation when the FTC would vanish for weeks or months at a time. The eerie uncertainty of silence was it's own torture. I'm not saying they inflicted it. I'm just saying it was a natural byproduct of having to wait. These are the moments I remember the most and wouldn't wish for anyone to experience. And that is also why I'm doing what I do now.

The money was the least of my concerns.

If I could go back in time and snap my fingers, I would wish that the investigation went faster, and I cut the check sooner and was done with it.

But, unfortunately that's not how it works.

And even though I dealt with a lot, it seems I was still better off than most. At times, my attorneys would become therapists. I'd get random calls to make sure I was hanging in there. I would get pep talks. I kept wondering why they called me so much, until I looked deeper into what had happened to entrepreneurs in the past.

So, what are the non-monetary costs of dealing with the FTC or any other government body?

Health

It turns out, the non-monetary cost of being investigated has no limit. In one case, it cost a man his life. One of the founders of MOBE (My Online Business Empire), Russ Whitney Jr., allegedly had a heart attack and died during an FTC investigation. He never even got to see how the case was resolved and passed away at the young age of 37.

Of course, I'm not insinuating that the FTC is going to kill you. But the stress and the risk of losing everything you've worked hard to build is enough stress to create many horrible health situations. In my own experience, I lost the ability to sleep for months. My chronic health condition flared for months at a time. I gained nearly 20 pounds. I lost all balance in my life. I was constantly distracted and stressed.

I had to add thousands of dollars of medications to fight back against the deteriorating health. All this while becoming a new father to two baby girls. Knowing that I couldn't afford to stress so much only made it worse.

Anxiety and depression almost took over my life, until I was finally able to get a handle on it. I credit my amazing wife, my family, my team, and my friends for all this. Not everyone is blessed with such an amazing environment, and without it, coping with an investigation is almost impossible.

I have hair that will never be black again. I have scars that will never heal again. I have PTSD that will take years to resolve. I have many health issues that will take time to recover, but when I sent the wire to the FTC, no one accounted for any of that.

Ironically, to me, that was the real cost.

Reputation Damage

Assuming that you've still got your health, your reputation is another big thing that the FTC can take away. They don't hide your case. Once you settle, they make it as public as they can.

The good news is that the investigation process (the CID) is confidential. The FTC, or other regulatory bodies, never publicly release anything. The only time things become public is if they choose to sue you, or you agree to a settlement.

The other thing that happens is that the FTC requires you to send a notice of the settlement to all your customers. Not only that, but after the settlement, the FTC themselves continue to message your customers for months, encouraging them to file claims for refunds.

The P.R. and "crisis control" can be a lot to manage. It was probably one of the hardest parts for me, mentally.

In my case, I chose not to hide my investigation from day one (even against legal advice). I spoke about it fairly openly, because frankly, I remain proud of the company I built. I felt that hiding things, and then having it hit the newswire suddenly and letting someone else tell my story, would do more damage.

But that didn't stop me from having near panic attacks about the day their press release would hit, the day the Industry would find out. I've seen quite a few of these press events go south for a brand very fast. Luckily for me, the goodwill of serving my Industry well for twenty years paid off.

But it doesn't for everyone.

Banking Challenges

Everyone in the financial world pays attention to FTC actions. Banks and merchant accounts get notified regularly of all FTC actions and are known to unscrupulously ban individuals who settle with the FTC. I had been warned about this from day one, so I had made my plans and communicated with all parties.

Luckily, I again was able to skate by without any major issues.

However, I did get a surprise letter from a bank that I won't name. I got a "we've terminated your account and you're no longer welcome to ever have an account with us" letter. Attached was a check for $3,600. The irony was, I had completely forgotten I even had this account, so for me, I appreciated them sending the money back.

The public shaming of a FTC settlement can be out of control, though. I have personally spoken to those who settled and who have faced interesting challenges, such as:

- Banned from opening bank accounts
- Trading accounts closed
- Denied gym memberships (yes, you read that right)
- Country club eviction
- Private school denied for children
- Removed from boards or companies they have equity in

As crazy as it is, the settlement or lawsuit becomes a permanent part of your identity, and it can take years to shake it off. Again, no one talks about this as a cost when settling with the FTC.

Injunctions & Bans

In my settlement, I was injuncted from making false statements. Basically, I am now enforced to follow the law, something we should all be doing anyways. However, many times, the person can be banned from an entire industry, or an entire type of business. Imagine if you've given your life to becoming excellent at one trade and are now banned for life from ever doing anything with it. You then need to start your life all over, a real risk you run if you're breaking the rules.

For example, Delray Capital was permanently banned from the debt collection industry for using robocalls and intimidating consumers into collecting "phantom debts." The FTC said they harassed people and pretended to be a mediation company, so they could collect money.

That's just one example out of hundreds.

Lawyer's Perspective

Greg Christiansen

Watching a client bear the burden of an investigation or regulatory lawsuit is difficult. Not only is the deck stacked against you, but you know that you will be outnumbered during the entire defense. That doesn't mean you don't fight. I will fight at every corner, if needed. But watching a client go through the process is like watching someone go through the stages of grief. At one point, they are very angry. The next moment, they are sad and depressed. It's a constant roller coaster.

With no shortage of absolutely horrible marketers with horrible intentions, sometimes the hardest part of a case is the "why me" factor. Sometimes, it's bad luck. Sometimes, it's the extreme aggressiveness of your marketing. Oftentimes, it is the volume of dissatisfied customers who believe they were misled. In Anik's case, it is difficult to understand. Generally, a business with little to no complaints, chargebacks, and/or refunds is not the first target of the FTC.

When the investigation or lawsuit hits, there is no time to think about the why. You have to go into defense mode. Part of my way of helping clients is to help them keep their perspective about things. I often turn into more of a therapist than an attorney. I try to get the client focused, which is sometimes difficult to do.

I admire the way that Anik handled the entire situation. Yes, he went through the phases of grief, and there were times I had to talk him down. But most of the time, he was reflective. How could he take this huge negative and make it a positive. I admire that.

My belief is that the monetary cost of the investigation is, of course, a painful one, but it's typically also a temporary one. You can always make more money. But the non-monetary cost of the investigation, and everything else that comes with it, can be life-long.

Obviously, there is life after the FTC, and I've seen many of my clients thrive and go on to do amazing things after their settlement. But I've also seen many clients crumble under the pressure and fade into nothingness.

So, yes, focusing on being compliant is not an option, it's an absolute necessity.

And when possible, I always strive for my client to reach a settlement.

Chapter 9:
How Do I Stay Off the Radar?

Greg Christiansen

My primary goal with my clients is to keep them off the "regulatory" bullseye or target. It's not really rocket science, or even fortune telling. Keeping businesses off the FTC's target is about understanding the rules and helping companies play within those parameters. Unfortunately, too many companies want to bury their heads in the sand, instead of learning how to compliantly sell a product or service.

What I do isn't magic. I've always liked the simple approach. I watch, listen, and read. I watch what the FTC does. I listen to what is being said in the industry. I read all of the cases and press releases. In my 20 years of doing this, what have I discovered?

Put simply—trends.

A majority of cases brought by the FTC in the past 20 years had beginnings based on the following five things:

1. Complaints
2. Business Associates
3. State-Level Investigations
4. Past Cases
5. Noncompliant Marketing

I am not claiming that this is a complete list. There could be some other way the FTC decides to bring an investigation or action, but these are generally the most common.

Complaints

In my experience, complaints are the primary attention getter. A loud complaining customer base can be the death knell. There is no magic number of complaints that gets you in trouble; it's all relative. I've even seen a single complaint get published in the national media and quickly create multiple lawsuits at many levels. A large number of complaints is usually a clear and strong indicator that your business has issues, and it's only a matter of time until the regulators take notice. Internal complaints, customer support complaints, BBB complaints, FTC complaints, and AG complaints are the biggest triggers for investigations.

In fact, it's a myth that your customers have to complain directly to the FTC for them to consider investigating you. That simply isn't true. The FTC shares a "complaint database" called Sentinel that compiles all company complaints with the BBB, the FTC, state departments, the Attorney General, and others. It's a tool that only the government has access to, not private attorneys.

Regulatory bodies track complaints. If they see a specific volume or type of complaint, they start digging. Here's a series of steps they will take if the complaints are getting to a significant volume:

1. They send a Civil Investigative Demand to obtain your bank records and figure out who your merchant processor is.
2. They issue an investigative demand to your payment processor. The request will ask about your chargebacks, refunds, and other complaints.
3. If the chargebacks come back over 2%, they start digging deeper.

Ultimately, this process could take a year or more before the FTC actually issues a CID or a lawsuit against you or the Company. Usually, by the time the FTC sends you a demand letter, they know most everything about your business. They have watched much of your advertising, read your sales pages, watched your webinars, read your emails, recorded sales calls, and embedded themselves in your funnel as a customer.

To protect yourself from this, limit your complaints.

And when you have a customer who is not happy, immediately take care of them. Do not give them the runaround. Do not refuse a refund on technical or contractual grounds. Build "quick and easy" refunds into your model and business plan, and you will save you a tremendous amount of pain.

However, as in the case of Anik and Lurn, a high number of complaints is not the only way to come under the regulatory radar. You can have low complaints, low chargebacks, and still become a target.

Business Associates

Unfortunately, when the FTC began their investigation against Anik's company, one of the very first things they wanted was a complete list of all partners, vendors, and affiliates. Basically, they wanted to know who had business dealings with his company.

There are multiple reasons for this. One is that they wanted to know who received profits from the business. First, the FTC wants to see if the owner has created multiple layers of businesses simply to shuffle money around in an attempt to hide ownership and assets. Second, the FTC wants to know who the affiliated businesses are that are supporting the company under investigation. Essentially, the FTC is looking to see who else needs to be included in the existing case, or if any new actions need to be brought against other companies.

This is common. When the FTC starts an investigation, they cast a wide net. Unbeknownst to you, there could be a company or person you're doing business with who has come under their radar. If that's the case, and you have earned any level of income from that business, your name will be revealed in documents.

This doesn't automatically mean that you'll be their next target. However, if your earnings are substantial, and your role is significant, then it's possible. This is why it's incredibly important to monitor who you do work with in the following ways:

- As an agency, monitor what your clients are doing.
- As an affiliate, make sure you are promoting compliant businesses.
- As a business partner, make sure you know the background and affairs of those you partner with.

Why? Because, in a way, their business is your business. You can't be ignorant to the problems of your "partners" or "third-party vendors." The FTC can attempt to bring an action against you by stating that "you knew or should have known" that the company you were doing business with was engaged in wrongful activities.

The FTC has used this approach multiple times to make a lawsuit or investigation (and eventually the settlement) bigger. Lately, they have even been hammering the payment processors, who they claim have knowledge of numerous complaints against a company, but continue to allow those companies to process money.

Getting investigated sometimes may not be about what you are doing directly, but what the company you partner with is doing.

State-Level Investigations

The FTC loves to tag-team with state agencies to bring actions. Operation Chokehold was a joint operation brought by the FTC and several states against merchant providers that were allowing "bad actors" to continue to collect payments from clients.

In FTC v. Ivy Capital, the FTC partnered with the Utah Division of Consumer Protection. In FTC v. Dalbey, the FTC partnered with the Colorado Attorney General. Recently, the FTC partnered with the state of Connecticut to launch an investigation against a Nissan dealership. Taking on two regulatory bodies at once makes the defense more challenging. In such cases, you will be facing both federal law and state law. If nothing else, a state regulatory issue certainly places a magnifying glass on you.

Past Cases & Business Partners

FTC settlements are called "Consent Judgments." Consent Judgments contain more than just the amount of the penalties and fines. These documents also include permanent injunctions and reporting requirements. Permanent injunctions may include prohibitions of the defendants from participating in specific activities, such as they:

- Can no longer make earnings claims
- Can no longer make misrepresentations
- Must have substantiation for all claims

In some cases, the prohibition can be far greater and more invasive creating a complete ban from:

- Seminar sales
- Telemarketing activities
- Participating in an entire industry (for example business opportunities)

In addition to injunctions, most FTC settlements have serious reporting requirements for up to 20 years that include always updating your contact information, informing the FTC of your business activities, and providing notification of your settlement to customers, employees, and contractors.

Most notably, post-settlement, the FTC watches your business more closely and keeps tabs on your activities. If you fail to follow every stipulation of your consent judgment, you are opening yourself up to further enforcement actions.

Recently, the FTC brought an additional action against the principles of Weblio. Two of the named individuals in the case were subject to prior regulatory actions. Now, just a few years later, they are in trouble with the FTC.

It seems like common sense, but sometimes people don't take the time to understand what they are agreeing to in the Consent Judgments, or worse they don't care. I know, it seems insane.

In this situation, the prior case of two of the principals could very well have put this business under additional supervision, and hence, put the other two partners at an increased risk. If your partner has had prior regulatory issues, you need to be sure that your current business is even more serious about compliance.

Noncompliant Marketing

You have to remember that, at the end of the day, the FTC is run by people. They are not robots. They live their lives, read mail, get email, watch television, and surf the Internet. They have Facebook, YouTube, Instagram, and TikTok accounts. Basically, they see your advertising in much the same way a "normal customer" would.

Perhaps they see very noncompliant marketing and decide to investigate further. Perhaps they have a disgruntled family member or friend who bought a "misleading product" from you. Sometimes, your marketing can just target the wrong person at the wrong time.

I know it sounds like the worst luck in the world, but it happens. More and more regulatory bodies are proactively conducting "search parties" and looking for marketing violations.

This is why the myth that only "large" businesses get sued is very wrong.

Yes, larger companies are subject to greater exposure. But most of the time, it's not because they are generating more money; it's because they're advertising more and have more visibility. So, unless you can find a magical way to make sure your ads are never seen by any regulator, or any friend or family member of the regulator, you're better off not trying to game the system, and instead, just follow the rules.

I want to repeat that these are not the only ways you can be found by the regulators. They just are the most common. The best medicine for every one of them?

Follow the rules and apply the methods we teach in this book.

Marketer's Perspective

Anik Singal

For ten years, I worried about the FTC because I knew I was in a heavily regulated industry. I worried about them so much that I spent over a million dollars in legal bills getting my systems, marketing, and other things reviewed.

I even hired a full-time paralegal in my company to listen to every sales call that led to a sale. I wanted to make sure nothing was being said that was unfair, unethical, or non compliant. Ironic, I know.

I built my company with the metrics I *thought* were being tracked by the FTC, such as complaint records, refund rates, merchant accounts, and reputation. And even though I excelled at all of those, in the end, it didn't matter.

My message to all marketers out there is that what I went through is not worth it at all. So, get compliant and use the right model to build your business, not the one you commonly see direct marketers using. Yes, it will take a little bit longer to hit your big goals, but you'll walk away with a far more solid business, better customers, and a business that can last decades, not months. A business built on compliant marketing is not just better from a regulation stand-point. It turns out, the business itself is a far better business.

Chapter 10:
An Overview of the
Investigative Process

Greg Christiansen

The investigative process is usually a multi-year process from beginning to end. This is important, because when you understand how the FTC works on the inside, you can better prepare and protect yourself.

For a moment, let's assume you have already landed on the FTC's radar. Here's how the ball gets rolling. There are a few stages the FTC will go through, and a few different options open to them. Typically, the investigation plays out like this:

1. Internal Investigation at the FTC
2. Warning Letter sent to company (not always)
3. Three possible outcomes
    a. CID
    b. Lawsuit
    c. TRO (Temporary Restraining Order) with asset freeze
4. Settlement or Lawsuit
5. Injunctive Relief
6. Press Release
7. Customer Notification

Internal Investigation

It all starts with an internal investigation. The regulators start looking into you, your business, and your associates to prepare an overall file. The goal here is to put together a report for the seniors at the agency to get the authorization, budget, and manpower approval needed to begin your investigation. The FTC, and other regulators, are definitely big agencies, but even they do not have unlimited resources.

The lawyers have to build a case and convince senior management of the worthiness of their preferred target. In the end, it's the decision of the Directors whether or not to authorize the investigation.

Many times, before you even receive your investigation document, regulators like the FTC have been looking into you, watching your marketing and building a case for at least a year. Assuming they get their approval, the next step may be a warning letter.

Warning Letter

This is new and not really required. However, under Section 5, if they want to be able to enforce fines for "web-driven one-to-many sales," a specific warning is required. They'll send you a letter warning you about some of the guidelines and rules. As of the writing of this, the warning letters are mostly generic. However, they do tip you off that you are being watched. Remember, if you have a one-to-one telesales team, the warnings are not required, and the FTC may jump straight to the next step.

The warning letters will re-summarize the laws but won't necessarily tell you what specific part of your advertising is breaking the law, or even if it's breaking the law. The letters tend to be more "for your information." The moment you get this letter, you need to make a major overhaul of your marketing.

The chances of you being investigated after receiving a warning letter go up dramatically. You're officially being watched. If within a few months you have not made monumental changes, the next step will be to send you a Civil Investigation Demand, or directly sue you.

CID

We've discussed this process above. It's grueling. It's long. It's expensive. It's thorough. They're going to send you a long letter demanding everything and anything they feel they need to investigate you. From financial records to all your marketing to all your communications. This process can take anywhere from a few months to years.

The more you deliver, the longer it will take, and the more thorough the FTC will be. During this process, the FTC assigns investigators to your case, in addition to the attorneys.

Lawsuit, TRO, Asset Freeze

If the FTC finds you to be very dangerous and significantly harming customers, they may skip the CID and go straight to a lawsuit. If they do that, it's very common for them to get a judge to sign off on a TRO (Temporary Restraining Order) and an asset freeze. This is by far the worst case scenario.

If you are using recurring sales or telephone sales, you should know that I'm still seeing TROs and asset freezes being granted by the courts.

If the FTC goes directly to a lawsuit, it's a completely different ballgame. You're in for a long fight, millions in costs, and a trying process. However, in a majority of the cases, the FTC first issues a CID and tries to settle. Again, yes they have a lot of resources, but they also have many companies they need to investigate. So, unless you're a very bad player, it's in their best interest to settle and move on.

Settlement or Lawsuit

After the investigation, the FTC delivers a Complaint Letter to you. This presents their findings and their case against you. In the letter, they'll make their first settlement offer or demand. They provide the terms, monetary numbers, and more.

Most of what they send has very little room for negotiation, except for their dollar figure, and even that isn't as much a negotiation as it is a justification. The only way to avoid paying the amount they demand is to show that you physically cannot afford to. If the amount is extremely high, it may make more sense to go to court.

Most cases settle. However, there are always the few rare cases where the parties cannot come to agreement, and the FTC will then move to lawsuit. Many clients will try to "bluff" and believe that, if they hold out and refuse to settle, the FTC will get tired and just let the case go. Believe me—this never happens.

If you don't settle, the FTC will absolutely go to court.

Injunctive Relief

The money is not the only penalty you pay. The terms of your settlement will involve other agreements, such as:

- Agreement to not break the rules you were accused of breaking
- Potential ban from a certain type of business or industry
- Customer notification terms
- Terms of transparency with employees, both present and future
- A number of years agreed for annual business reporting requirements

These terms can be exhaustive in some cases, and at times, even more troubling than the monetary fine.

Press Release

This is the dreaded announcement to the world, when the FTC will issue a press release, tweets, articles, and more about your case. These almost always go viral and get picked up fast. The more of a public figure you are, the more media your story will attract.

Unfortunately, the FTC is not kind in these articles. The press releases are normally written in a fashion that makes it sound like you were tried and found guilty (regardless of your lack of admission or trial). The press releases are also a surprise. You are not given any say, feedback, or notice.

These releases can be very damaging to brands and the online records are permanent.

Customer Notification

Typically, within a period of seven days from the judge signing off on the settlement agreement, you're not only required to send the wire, but you need to send an email to all your customers. The FTC is kind enough to type this email for you and asks that you send it verbatim.

As you can imagine, this requires you to be prepared to do some damage control.

Customers can become concerned and may have many questions. A company needs to prepare ahead of time to handle this matter delicately. However, your notification to the customers will not be the only one.

Post-settlement, when you send the money to the FTC, they will also send their own notifications to each customer. They will ask all customers to file their claims for a refund. They send these notifications from their systems, and they get to say whatever they want. It is out of your hands. This can go on for months, which means the PR impact of a settlement can last quite some time.

Marketer's Perspective

Anik Singal

Exhausting. Brutal. Long. Painful. Horrible.

The list of words to explain this process is endless. My biggest advice to anyone who gets a warning letter is to get a lawyer immediately. Stop your business immediately. Track every single step you take in response to the warning letter. Only turn your business back on if you know you are 100% compliant. If you're not able to get to 100% compliance, immediately shut the business down forever.

If you react very strongly to the warning letter, you could end up saving yourself a lot of trouble.

My advice to you if you get a CID is to brace for impact. You're guilty. Sorry to strip you of any hope, but the work your lawyers are doing now is just to minimize the damage, not avoid it. My best advice to you?

- Don't let it stretch out.
- End it quickly.
- Turn over documents quickly.
- Move to negotiations quickly.
- Band Aid – rip it and let it burn.

The longer you stretch it out, the more painful, the more impactful, and the more expensive it will be. That is one thing I would change about my case. I would have inquired about what I could do to make it go faster. The extra time didn't really help; it only ended up costing me more.

I just hope that you follow everything we teach in this book and never ever get a warning letter or a CID.

Part 3:
How To Comply

Chapter 11:
Breaking Down The Rules

Greg Christiansen

Compliance is a web. Several elements are interconnected. You go down one path, and it intersects with another. It has taken me 20 years and studying literally hundreds of cases to figure out what the FTC and state governments want and don't want.

The problem is that there is no clear road map on what does and doesn't constitute a violation. Yes, I know there is the FTC Act, and there are various rules, such as the Testimonial and Endorsement Guidelines, but the application of those rules is sometimes fuzzy.

That is why I focus on cases. I try to read and analyze every judgment or settlement obtained by the FTC. Cases are my roadmap to insights into the FTC and their interpretation of the FTC Act. I've studied hundreds of cases.

This is the simplest way I know how to compress twenty years of experience into a single book.

1. The Pentagon of Compliance

This is a term I came up with. It isn't everything, but it contains the "core" essentials of what I believe are the biggest issues the FTC and regulatory bodies focus on.

The Pentagon of Compliance

2. Universal Violations

Another term of mine, these rules apply to every type of marketing, including sales pages, webinars, video sales letters, one-on-one tele-sales, and anything else you can think of.

3. Specifics

I want to drive attention to each of these types of marketing channels, specifically. There are certain things that a telesales call must have that don't apply to written sales pages, so we'll make those distinctions.

We're going to talk about each of these types of marketing:

- Written sales pages
- Videos or Webinars
- Telesales
- Recurring sales

Remember, don't shoot the messenger. The rules are the rules. Neither I, nor Anik, made them. The good news is the power you get when you understand the rules. When you truly understand that playing within the sandbox is not a bad thing at all—it's an advantage.

Marketer's Perspective

Anik Singal

My entire perspective is more about how shocked I was to learn what all the rules were. No one teaches these! I would even argue that a large majority of attorneys don't even know them.

Most marketers that are in business right now are thinking that they're perfectly compliant. Most marketers think their lack of complaints is an iron-clad shield. Yet, they have no idea that their company may currently be up on a projector inside the FTC office. The education you're about to receive comes from an attorney who has read pretty much every case the FTC has closed in the last 20 years.

What you're about to hear is not published anywhere else in such a concise and easy-to-understand way. Also, get ready to be a bit frustrated. Getting compliant means you're going to have to change many things. It's not easy. Your first reaction is going to be to think that marketing compliantly is not possible. I can tell you with a lot of confidence that, if you commit to it, compliant marketing is not only possible—it builds a much stronger business.

The problem is, it's been decades of marketers copying each other and stacking on top of their predecessors. And this has all led to some very bad habits that now need to be unlearned.

Chapter 12:
Misrepresentations

Greg Christiansen

Let's dive in and get started. The first side of the Pentagon of Compliance is Misrepresentations. It's simple. Make sure your marketing is truthful and accurate. Don't lie. Don't say things that aren't true. Don't imply things that mislead. Don't misrepresent. Don't be tricky.

The Pentagon of Compliance

Ever caught someone in the middle of something and asked them, "You didn't tell me you were doing this," only to get the reply, "Well, you didn't ask."

Don't Say That

How frustrating is that?

Well, the FTC doesn't play these games. It's common sense that lying is bad. But this is where marketers try to get creative. They decide to bend the truth or walk around it.

It doesn't matter if you don't specifically say the wrong thing. To the regulators, it's the same if you strategically leave things out, and in doing so, implying them.

Here's nine of the most common types of misrepresentations I see:

1. A.I. bots & fake profiles
2. Fake sales & discounts
3. Implying connection to someone famous
4. Success story creation
5. Fake live webinars
6. Environmental claims
7. Health-related claims
8. Made in the USA claims

Let's take a closer look at each of these to see why they're problematic.

A.I. bots & fake profiles
The use of A.I. in customer interactions is a new thing, but that doesn't mean the FTC isn't paying attention. The rules are still being developed, but we expect there to be many moves in the world of regulating A.I.

The FTC is approaching this by combining a few things. For instance, they're linking it to the Telephone Consumer Protection Act (TCPA). According to the TCPA, you need consent (opt-ins) from clients to call or text them using bots.

Also, the use of other forms of A.I. is increasingly being reviewed. In January 2024, the FTC held a conference dedicated to the use of A.I. in marketing. The FTC is closely monitoring the use of AI, including the manipulation of images and voices, which will likely become a significant concern in the future.

Think about it this way?. If an A.I. bot places a phone call to a consumer and says, "Hi, I'm Jack from Acme, Inc.," the entire call is a misrepresentation in the first five words. Will it be required that an A.I. bot identify itself as such? Other issues, such as ringless voicemails and other uses of A.I., are going to fall under increased scrutiny and review.

New rules and regulations about how to use A.I. in marketing are definitely going to come soon. We will keep you updated through our podcast at DontSayThat.com.

Fake sales & discounts
Discounting is normal. Everybody does it. The problem comes when the discounts aren't real. They are randomly made up. *"The knowledge in this PDF is worth at least $1,997!"* I always ask, "How did you get to that number?"

If you can't prove the value of your services, then you also can't "slash prices" and offer it to a customer for a discount. Take this example:

"Learn the secrets of real estate investing! Masterclass A, valued at $2,000, now $499."

The problem with this is that the marketer is valuing the Masterclass at $2,000. Who said it was worth $2,000? Did you sell a justifiable number of the same classes at $2,000? If not, you can't claim and substantiate the $2,000 value, and the claim is a misrepresentation.

The FTC will want substantiation of the price, which can only occur when you've sold many copies at that exact price. Again, I can see a marketer's "creative mind" turning on, so let me address it head on.

No. A single sale to your best friend at $2,000 is not enough. It needs to be a reasonable number of real sales. You can't just get a few people to buy it at $2,000 and convince the FTC it's worth $2,000.

In summary, if you're going to offer discounts or make value claims, make sure you have ample substantiation and have sold many copies at the original price.

Implying connection to someone famous
There were many cases in the past of influencers getting paid to make an ad for a product that they had barely ever held in their hands, much less used. There are two parts to this:

1. Using an influencer's picture and video without their permission.
2. Paying an influencer for some pictures, then pretending they're your #1 customer.

The first one is not only going to get you in trouble with the regulators, but it's going to get you sued by the person whose face you are using. I've seen this far too many times. I see marketers using "brand association" all the time.

Years ago, I had a client who promoted their own product by offering free tickets to go see a very heavily promoted Indiana Jones movie. *"Buy my product, get some free tickets."*

Innocent right?

Well, it was an illegal brand association. Customers felt more credibility towards the brand by it leaning on the credibility of the Indiana Jones franchise, without relationship or authorization. My conversation with Paramount's General Counsel was not pleasant, to say the least.

I see marketers use pictures of celebrities many times. You go to an event and get a chance to take a picture with a well known speaker, and suddenly, that picture becomes an advertisement. Again, you're asking for trouble.

As for the second, here is another clear misrepresentation. You pay an influencer for a shoutout on their social media, but you make it look as if they are doing it on their own. They just felt compelled to talk about your product. This will be seen as deceptive in the eyes of the regulators.

Seeing your favorite celebrity promoting a product gives that product instant credibility in your mind. The average consumer does not immediately think the celebrity may have been paid for it. They genuinely believe the celebrity trusts the brand and uses it. If this is not true, and all you did was send some money and a sample product for the photograph, it's a clear misrepresentation and is illegal.

A perfect example of this was the FTC vs Lord & Taylor. The FTC accused Lord & Taylor of being deceptive when the company paid 50 influencers up to $4,000 each to post pictures of them wearing their clothes. The problem was that these influencers were paid, yet there were no disclosures made that it was a paid advertisement.

Success story creation
In other words, "We need you to become a success story..."

Bill, you've got to join us. We're specifically looking for our next 10 success stories. We want to be able to use your story in our marketing. Scratch that, we need to use your story in our marketing, so we're going to give it all we got. You're going to get VIP treatment. Let's get you to become a success

Don't Say That

story fast, so we can tell the world. We'll help you. You'll help us. We're in this together."

I cannot tell you how many sales calls I have listened to where this is being said. Look, it sounds great, but you and I both know, it's just not true.

That sales call is likely the 687th call that one sales agent has made, and the team has seven other agents. Every single consumer is being told they're going to get this hyper special attention because the company is relying on them to be the next big success story for them.

This is a clear misrepresentation.

For starters, they're not going to get any VIP treatment that any normal customer isn't getting. Misrepresentation #1.

Next, the company has no way to track or validate the "next 10." Misrepresentation #2.

Next, the company is making an inflated claim of needing their story for the company's survival. Misrepresentation #3.

It's an innocent thing in the minds of many of my clients. *"What? We're just telling them that we're rooting for them and will help them as much as we can."*

No, you're not. You're misrepresenting the level of importance they will carry for you. You're making them feel special, which in return, becomes a very big part of their buying decision.

Classic misrepresentation.

Fake live webinars

If you've ever run live webinars, then repurposed them as evergreen, you're technically misrepresenting. This was actually flagged in Anik's case.

- *"We have 1,200 people on!"* If you're evergreen, no you don't.
- *"Samatha, I see your comment!"* If you're evergreen, no you don't.
- *"Wow, the comments are flying in."* If you're evergreen, you can't see comments.

Basically, you're pretending you're LIVE in an evergreen webinar, and some consumers are going to get duped and believe you. Hence, you're misrepresenting.

Even worse, you may have offered a discount or a limited time bonus on the LIVE webinar when you recorded it. Technically, you are now taking that same recording and offer and making it evergreen. So, essentially, you lied on the LIVE webinar—that bonus or price really wasn't limited at all.

I think it's obvious how this is an issue.

Of course, I understand why marketers do this. Filming a webinar with a LIVE audience leads to a better recording; the energy feels different. So, my suggestion is to go ahead and use the LIVE recording as an evergreen, but it has to be clear that it is a recording. Consequently, you have to avoid the following when you're doing the actual LIVE webinar:

- Calling out names
- Pretending you have a swarm of responses
- Doing limited time bonuses or pricing
- Doing a Q&A where you make it look spontaneous and call names

Don't Say That

If you clearly disclose that the presentation the client is watching is recorded, you can do all of the above. But if the presentation looks like it's live when it's actually a recording, it's a misrepresentation. You can still ask for engagement. You just can't pretend to see that people are engaging back in return. This may sound like it'll hurt the conversions a lot, but ask Anik. He's been able to do this, and the conversions on the evergreen remained great.

As a matter of fact, he's even leaned into it and been up-front lately that what they're watching is NOT LIVE.

Environmental claims
Claims about environmental benefits (product or packaging) must be supported by competent and reliable scientific evidence. The FTC released a "Green Guide" that helps marketers understand when they can use the environmentally friendly claims. Going back to 1992, these rules outline what you can and can't say in your marketing.

In 2022, the FTC sued Kohl's and Walmart for marketing dozens of rayon textile products as eco-friendly bamboo. Both companies allegedly said that the "bamboo" textiles were made using eco-friendly processes, but in reality, converting bamboo into rayon requires the use of toxic chemicals and pollutes the environment. So, their products were actually the opposite of eco-friendly.

Basically, if you don't have scientific proof that your product is "green," don't use this kind of language. If you want to help out the environment, great. But don't lie to your customers.

Health-related claims
Companies marketing food, drugs, dietary supplements, and health-related products must back their advertising claims with solid proof. You need to run studies that are peer-reviewed and done by third parties.

Making any form of health claims can get you in trouble, not only with the FTC, but the FDA.

The FTC works with the FDA, but the FTC is primarily in charge of the advertising side of things. That being said, if your product is not FDA approved and you're making claims of treating an illness or even curing it, it's a very fast way to get the attention of the FTC.

As a matter of fact, in April 2023, the FTC issued a warning to nearly 700 supplement and health companies (including companies like Merck, Pfizer, and other public companies). They reminded them of the rules for marketing health products and clearly said they will begin regulating aggressively.

Made in the USA claims
Products promoted as "Made in the USA" must comply with FTC's "Made in USA" Labeling Rule. The policy says that a product has to be entirely or almost entirely made in the United States to be eligible, and that the claim of "Made in the USA" has to be substantiated.

In May 2023, the FTC settled with "Lions Not Sheep" for $176,000 for allegedly "ripping off 'Made in China' tags and replacing them with 'Made in USA' tags." The company ended up refunding 11,512 customers, who bought their shirts.

Even companies as big as Williams-Sonoma have had to settle with the FTC for similar mistakes. In March 2020, Wiliams-Sonoma agreed to settle for $1 million for a line of their products that claimed to be "Made in the USA," but was actually imported.

Small and big companies alike, the FTC is very serious about any kind of misrepresentation made to consumers.

Marketer's Perspective

Anik Singal

I find this to be the easiest one. Don't lie. Don't pretend. Don't exaggerate. I'm good with that. There were a few here that caught my attention, though. The ones I thought would be fairly innocent.

Using a LIVE webinar as an evergreen and pretending to have an audience isn't one I would have thought to be a big enough problem to make it into my complaints, but it did.

The other one that shocked me was that offering to help someone become a case study and making them feel special is frowned upon. Of course, when I looked at it through the eyes of the regulators, I immediately saw the issue.

However, at face value, most marketers would never equate those things to "breaking the law."

This is exactly why I wanted Greg to write this book with me. The rules are just never talked about, until it's too late.

Chapter 13:
It All Starts & Ends with "Net Impression"

Greg Christiansen

Net Impression might be the most misunderstood concept in marketing. Net Impression is the second wall in the Compliance Pentagon. It is the "catch all" law that protects against marketers trying to "game" the law or find loopholes. Having been an attorney behind the scenes on many investigations, I can tell you that the term "Net Impression" comes up a lot behind the scenes.

The bottomline is this. Forget the specifics. Forget the rules. Forget the disclosures. Forget the details. Think about just one thing—after watching your sales presentation, what is the "net impression" on the average prospect? Do they believe that buying your product will make them $10,000 by next month? Or that buying your product will help them get six-pack abs by next week?

Sure, you didn't actually say it. But would a reasonable consumer believe that?

If the answer is yes, you are not compliant.

The Pentagon of Compliance

- 1 MISREPRESENTATION
- 2 NET IMPRESSION
- 3 CLAIMS
- 4 SUBSTANTIATION
- 5 TESTIMONIALS

(COMPLIANCE at the center)

Let's say you're in a room, and everyone is introducing themselves...

- Person #1 says they're a multi-millionaire in the banking industry.
- Person #2 says they're a multi-millionaire in the banking industry.
- Person #3 says they're a multi-millionaire in the banking industry.
- Person #4, says the same thing.
- Person #5, says the same thing.
- Person #6, same...
- Person #7, same...

If you were a betting person in Vegas, what would you bet Person #8 is? A multi-millionaire in the banking industry?

That is the "Net Impression."

This is why the FTC asks for typical results testimonials only. When you layer in testimonial after testimonial after testimonial of huge results, no matter how much you disclaim, the regulators believe that the average consumer walks away with a net impression that they will earn that much too.

Basically, the net impression of an advertisement is the overall takeaway that customers are left with. The FTC puts itself in the shoes of a reasonable consumer, and then they look at all your ads, including words, images, videos, etc. I always tell clients context is king. It's not just the words used, but all the other elements around the specific words.

If you shoot a YouTube video saying "anyone can do this," while in front of a Lamborghini, it's different from shooting it in front of a park or a typical street corner. Sure, you could use a "results not typical" disclaimer, and you should, but if everything else is violating the rules, the disclaimer alone will not protect you because the context of what you're saying may be non-disclaimable.

Because of the net impression rule, you have to be that much more careful with the sales messaging you're putting out there. This is exactly why a legal review is so important. A compliance attorney, such as myself (with years of specific experience), is trained to know how to put ourselves in the shoes of the regulators and read your advertisements. Also, some of the rules are written in a way that there is no black or white; the gray always comes down to the net impression.

In some cases, you may be able to say one thing, whereas in other cases, the same thing won't be allowed. Why? The context in which it is said, and the net impression it creates.

The point I want to get across is that the FTC and other regulators don't look at isolated words or phrases in a literal sense. They consider the entire message as a whole. Their main goal is to make sure the consumer is not being misled into making a purchase.

One of the examples the FTC uses when explaining net impression is the 1987 press release from a book publisher. Georgetown Publishing House sent out a bunch of snail mail letters that were designed to look like book reviews. Their creativity got the better of them when they added what looked like a personalized note endorsing the book they were promoting. The FTC said it was false advertising because it created the net impression that the review was impartial.

They needed to make it clear that the mailer was an advertisement.

We can see this same thing in the more recent case against Lord & Taylor, where they didn't disclose that their influencers were being paid to wear their clothing. The net impression was that the influencers had chosen to wear the clothes on their own, and were so happy they went out of their way to post their content. However, the truth was that they were paid.

So…

Net impression = They loved it so much, they made a video
Truth = They were given money, so they made the content

Another example is one I see everyday. The marketers who display "money guns," like Lamborghinis, yachts, and private jets in the background. They're living "the life" and talking in their video about how they've broken the code to riches.

Obviously, the rich life background is creating a net impression that investing in their opportunity is going to give the consumer a quick way to get the same life. It also gives the net impression that they own those assets. However, many times, they don't. They rented them for that photo or video shoot.

Sure, there is no law in the FTC Act that says you can't film with fancy cars. But the net impression the client walks away with ends up being very different from what the true average results are.

A perfect example is the Ab Circle Pro case. Here you have the now late Suzane Summers using a machine to do just 10 sit ups, then you see her world-class bodybuilder abs. The impression left was that, in less than 10 minutes a day, you can have an eight pack. In the end, most customers complained that they felt deceived by the impression of extreme ease.

Another example is the "Shape Up Shoes" by Sketchers. Wear these wedged shaped shoes and you (ads directly mostly to women) will have toned legs and glutes. Again, many wished it was true, but alas, it was another misleading net impression.

So, how does net impression relate to your ad copy or your sales copy?

Moving forward, all the "rules" we discuss come in second to net impression. Please remember that if you try to "get around the rules," but keep the same underlying meaning or purpose of your marketing, the law covers itself using net impression. Net Impression is the very heart of Section 5 of the FTC Act, which literally commissioned the formation of the FTC to begin with.

As a matter of fact, if you ever want to answer your own compliance questions, just ask yourself, "Does the thing I'm about to say create a false net impression?" You'll answer your own question.

Ultimately, "how a consumer perceives something" can appear to be very subjective, but the law tries to put it into the context of a "reasonable person" and they get to define "reasonable." Rather than taking your chances arguing with the regulators or judges, you're better off getting a lawyer who can think like these regulators to review your marketing and tell you your net impression.

Marketer's Perspective

Anik Singal

I became friends with a great marketer, let's call him Marty (protecting his identity out of respect). Marty was being investigated by the FTC at the same time I was. Their line of business was a bit different, but we shared some similarities. Their case ended in a settlement, as well, a few months before mine.

In his case, after the settlement was inked and done, they had a debriefing call with the FTC. During the call, the FTC attorneys wrapped up their entire advice to the company by saying (and I'm paraphrasing), "Look, moving forward, it's all about the net impression. If your copy makes it feel like promises are made that can't be substantiated, or that results are guaranteed even if you don't say it, well, then you're in violation. Focus on the net impression. Let that guide you."

Now, I didn't hear this with my own ears, but I trust "Marty." Imagine that. Their final closing words in a case. Sounds important to me, no?

Chapter 14:
Earnings Claims

Greg Christiansen

The Pentagon of Compliance

Claims are the third item on the Pentagon of Compliance. This is anything from "Here's how to make $32,000 a month with no experience" (earnings claim) to "How to get six-pack abs in just 7 minutes a day" (performance claim) to "Reclaim your time and become a member of the financial freedom club" (lifestyle claim).

As you can see, claims do not have to be just about money. Here's some other examples:

- "Here's how to lose 25 pounds in 30 days eating anything you want."
- "How to find your soulmate in 7 days or less."
- "How to live stress free, find financial freedom, and become your own boss."

All these are claims that need to be substantiated and proven. Be honest. How many times a day do you see marketing messages with such specific promises? It's so often that it's become normal for us. As a matter of fact, most of us have started to think this is good marketing. That leads one marketer to copy another and the problem snowballs.

Now, go back and read the claims again, but put on a different "hat." I do this all the time. I'll look at an ad from different perspectives, as an attorney, a buyer, and sometimes even as my late 86-year-old mother. And yes, even through the eyes of an FTC regulator. I can usually immediately see where the problems are. If the claims seem outlandish to me, they'll seem outlandish to someone else. Factually speaking, you have zero control over any results anyone else gets. And if you claim to, you better have tons of proof to back up that claim.

The examples I gave you are pretty obvious. However, the FTC rules regarding claims go a bit deeper. There are four types of claims the FTC evaluates:

1. Express earnings claims
2. Implied earnings claims
3. Lifestyle claims
4. Performance claims

Let's dive into each one in detail.

Express earnings claims

Express earnings claims are explicit statements made about specific monetary outcomes someone can expect to get by purchasing a program. The examples we started with are examples of specific promises:

- Make $32,000...
- Start making $1,000 a day...
- How to build a $1 million business from home...

The problem is that marketers are making these claims out of thin air. Maybe they themselves had those results, but they're providing no context. It may have taken them years of failing and experience to get those results. Also, have a majority of their customers had the same results? Are the specific results they're claiming typical?

The truth is that 99% of the time the FTC knows these claims are not substantiated or typical, and this gives the regulators an easy door to walk through. They can use these claims as a way to start their investigation.

The Digital Altitude case is a perfect example. They sold training packages that promised their customers they would earn "six figures in just 90 days." This is a textbook express earnings claim. And of course, the lion's share of their customers never got even close to those results. Complaints from customers prompted an FTC investigation. This ended with multiple founders having to settle, getting injunctions and paying a total of nearly $4.7 million in refunds to customers.

3	**COUNT I**
4	**Misrepresentations Regarding Earnings**
5	67. In numerous instances in connection with the advertising, marketing,
6	promotion, offering for sale, or sale of their purported money-making
7	opportunities, Defendants have represented, directly or indirectly, expressly or by
8	implication, that purchasers of their purported money-making opportunities would
9	earn or were likely to earn substantial income, such as six figures in ninety days or
10	less.
11	68. Defendants' representations set forth in Paragraph 67 of this
12	Complaint are false, misleading, or were not substantiated at the time the
13	representations were made.
14	69. Therefore, Defendants' representations as set forth in Paragraph 67 of
15	this Complaint constitute a deceptive act or practice in or affecting commerce in
16	violation of Section 5(a) of the FTC Act, 15 U.S.C. § 45(a).

Case Summary

The Federal Trade Commission alleged that the defendants operated a multi-million dollar business coaching scheme known as Digital Altitude that they deceived consumers by claiming they could earn "six figures in 90 days."

The Federal Trade Commission is sending refunds totaling nearly $4.7 million to people who lost money as a result of the scheme.

Image source: FTC (2019)[2]

If you look at the case summary, you can tell that the central thing the FTC focused on was the line *"six figures in 90 days."*

Implied earnings claims

Implied earnings claims are more subtle than express earnings claims, but they're just as regulated. However, they can be harder to identify. But if you know the rules behind them, they are easy to spot. They paint a picture of success without explicitly promising a specific result.

---

[2] FTC. 2019. Digital Altitude LLC. https://www.ftc.gov/legal-library/browse/cases-proceedings/172-3060-x180021-digital-altitude-llc

Basically, the claims imply that someone can expect a certain level of monetary gain, without specifically stating it. So, if an express earnings claim sounds like "Six figures in 90 days," an implied earnings claim might be a series of checks that show big money or the use of multiple testimonials that show big income.

Many marketers love to try to game the system. They will say, "Well, I didn't 'say' anything or even imply anything. I used truthful testimonials I got from my customers, where they talk about their own results."

Simple, right? Not at all. They are violating that net impression rule, and the statements, imagery, and examples are all making the client believe they will get the same exact results.

Of course, you can publish someone else's results (claim) in your marketing. However, you still need to substantiate that claim yourself, their word is not enough. Also, you still need to make sure that the result is the typical result of a typical customer, you cannot cherry pick the best and present them.

Another perfect example of an implied earnings claim is the Advocare case, which led to $149 million being returned to consumers. Advocare is a billion dollar annual business, who at the time, had a multilevel marketing division that sold and distributed dietary products. They promoted it as a very successful business opportunity for anyone.

They relied heavily on implied earnings claims through testimonials. Here's what the FTC had to say…

> opportunity purportedly available through AdvoCare. Defendants have published thousands of deceptive income claims, and the below claims are mere examples of their conduct:
>
> a. In an August 2018 recruiting video that the company posted on its Facebook and YouTube pages, an AdvoCare General Manager said that she asks consumers, "What's that amount per month that you'd like to earn? And then a year from now let's look at that and let's decide: is that the same amount or maybe you want to give yourself a raise? The great thing about owning your own business is that you can." She then showed a graphic of a Distributor with annual earnings of more than $413,000, which she referred to as "astounding income." Closing the video, she stated that if consumers wanted "a part-time income . . . a full-time income, [had] a desire to be at home with your family, a desire to travel, or to be able to take your family on trips—whatever reason . . . a year from now you will wish you had started today."

Image source: FTC (2019)[3]

Overnight, Advocare shut down its MLM division, eliminating thousands of distributors in the process. They had over $1 billion to their name, so a $149 million fine was not the end of them. However, in my experience, many clients can't even afford a $100,000 fine without being devastated.

Lifestyle claims

Alright. No express earnings claims. Check. No implied earnings claims. Check.

Here comes the "Mr. Creative Marketer" with a sales message that is full of videos and images of luxury cars, mansions, and private jets. Technically, you're not providing dollar amounts, but in the eyes of the FTC, to the average consumer, the misleading message is loud and clear…

---

[3] FTC. 2019. United States District Court for the Eastern District of Texas Sherman Division. https://www.ftc.gov/system/files/documents/cases/advocare_complaint_0.pdf.

"You too can immediately have these expensive cars and houses if you buy my product."

As long as your typical customer is driving a Bentley and living in a mansion, thanks to your product, go ahead, market away. But if your typical customer is not a high-flying millionaire, don't use these props to inflate your marketing.

> 33. In addition to the spoken content, the live presentations at Defendants' events often involve images of expensive houses, luxury automobiles, and exotic vacations.

Image Source: FTC (2016)[4]

> 22. In some but not all instances, Defendants accompany their misleading income representations with purported "disclaimers." These purported disclaimers, which often appear in small print, do not alter the net impression created by Defendants' misleading representations, namely, that Distributors are likely to earn substantial income. (See, for example, the graphic illustration at Paragraph 37, which contains the following disclaimer: "Incomes applicable to the individuals (or examples) depicted and not average. For average financial performance data, see the Statement of Average Gross Compensation of U.S. Supervisors at Herbalife.com and MyHerbalife.com.")

Image Source: FTC (2017)[5]

Both of these are screenshots from the FTC discussion of their case against Herbalife. They go out of their way to mention all the lifestyle claims. And it's not just this case. The FTC has countless cases where they

---

[4] FTC. 2019. United States District Court Central District of California. Case No. 2:16-cv-05217. https://www.ftc.gov/system/files/documents/cases/160715herbalifecmpt.pdf.
[5] FTC. 2017. Redress checks and compliance checks: Lessons from the FTC's Herbalife and Vemma cases. https://www.ftc.gov/business-guidance/blog/2017/01/redress-checks-and-compliance-checks-lessons-ftcs-herbalife-and-vemma-cases.

show their disdain for flashy cars, mansions, watches, yachts, jets, and the like. The FTC also looks at representations, such as "quit your day job," "become your own boss," and "obtain the financial freedom and time freedom you deserve."

The best way to avoid problems with lifestyle claims is to think about your visuals and what you're promoting. Target your average customer. Think about the net impression. And if you feel like you might have to ask a lawyer if a certain image or video is okay, my experience says that odds are, it's not.

Performance claims
A performance claim is when you say that your product or service will enhance performance, usually in the fitness or wellness space. This generally is there for health companies, supplement brands, weight loss products, beauty products, and the like.

This one has nothing to do with monetary gain but rather performance…

- Lose 30 pounds in 30 days.
- Get six-pack abs.
- Find your soul mate in 7 days or less.

If you say your supplement can lead to rapid weight loss, that's a performance claim. If you say your skincare cream can make customers look ten years younger, that's another one. One example was Lumos Labs, the creators of the "Lumosity" brain training program. In 2016, the FTC said Lumosity told people their app could improve performance in school and work and reduce age-related cognitive decline. The FTC stepped in and said that there was no substantiation or proof of this claim.

Lumosity had to settle for $2 million, and was required to notify its subscribers about the settlement, giving them an immediate and easy way to cancel their membership.

Earnings Claims

> The creators and marketers of the Lumosity "brain training" program have agreed to settle Federal Trade Commission charges alleging that they deceived consumers with unfounded claims that Lumosity games can help users perform better at work and in school, and reduce or delay cognitive impairment associated with age and other serious health conditions.
>
> As part of the settlement, Lumos Labs, the company behind Lumosity, will pay $2 million in redress and will notify subscribers of the FTC action and provide them with an easy way to cancel their auto-renewal to avoid future billing.

Image Source: FTC (2016)[6]

COUNT I

FALSE OR UNSUBSTANTIATED REAL-WORLD PERFORMANCE CLAIMS

26. Through the means described in Paragraph 18, Defendants have represented, directly or indirectly, expressly or by implication, that training with the Lumosity Program provides real-world benefits for users by:

    A. Improving performance on everyday tasks;

    B. Improving performance in school;

    C. Improving performance at work; and

    D. Improving athletic performance.

27. The representations set forth in Paragraph 26 are false or were not substantiated at the time the representations were made.

Image Source: FTC (2016)[7]

As a matter of fact, the FTC regularly goes after supplement and health-related brands. Income claims are not their only focus and are only a percentage of their cases.

---

[6] FTC. 2016. Lumosity to Pay $2 million to Settle FTC Deceptive Advertising Charges for Its "Brain Training" Program. https://www.ftc.gov/news-events/news/press-releases/2016/01/lumosity-pay-2-million-settle-ftc-deceptive-advertising-charges-its-brain-training-program.

[7] FTC. 2019. United States District Court for the Northern District of California San Francisco Division. https://www.ftc.gov/system/files/documents/cases/160105lumoslabscmpt.pdf

Don't Say That

The regulators are looking for any and all unsubstantiated claims. In fact, "false and unsubstantiated earnings claims" is the number one legal theory the FTC uses against marketers selling a money making opportunity. For example, in the Automators case, this is the first cause of action:

3	**COUNT I**
4	**Misrepresentations Regarding Earnings**
5	67. In numerous instances in connection with the advertising, marketing,
6	promotion, offering for sale, or sale of their purported money-making
7	opportunities, Defendants have represented, directly or indirectly, expressly or by
8	implication, that purchasers of their purported money-making opportunities would
9	earn or were likely to earn substantial income, such as six figures in ninety days or
10	less.
11	68. Defendants' representations set forth in Paragraph 67 of this
12	Complaint are false, misleading, or were not substantiated at the time the
13	representations were made.
14	69. Therefore, Defendants' representations as set forth in Paragraph 67 of
15	this Complaint constitute a deceptive act or practice in or affecting commerce in
16	violation of Section 5(a) of the FTC Act, 15 U.S.C. § 45(a).

Image source: FTC (2018)[8]

Notice that it's not just false earnings claims, but also unsubstantiated claims. This means, as we discuss substantiation in the next chapter, that even if a claim really is true, you have to be able to prove it.

What if I CAN Back Up My Claim?

If you're thinking, "Okay, I get the part about not lying to people. But what if what I'm saying is true? What if I can back it up?"

Let's say you used a certain supplement and actually lost 30 pounds since you started using it? You have proof. Why can't you say that? If you have

---

[8] FTC. 2018. United States District Court Central District of California. https://www.ftc.gov/system/files/documents/cases/digital_altitude_complaint.pdf

absolute proof of your own results, you can mention your own results with a lot of context, making it clear you are using it solely as a source of credibility. However, if you start leaning heavily on your own results, even if proven, you are going to create a net impression problem.

So, what are you supposed to sell, if you can't sell claims?

This is where most marketers argue with me. They say, "How can I sell anyone anything if I can't sell them the dream?"

My argument is simply this. I have many clients who sell millions and millions a year without breaking the rules. You can sell your education, but you can't sell the results, unless you have proof that the results are typical. Period.

Ferrari can sell you a car that's fast, and they're welcome to say that (it's substantiated). However, what they can't sell you is the impression that you will win the next Formula One trophy.

And by the way, if using results-based testimonials and marketing is vital to your business, you have one option that allows you to use them. It won't be easy, but it unlocks this for you. We'll discuss how to do this later in the chapter.

Marketer's Perspective

Anik Singal

I have so much to say here, I don't know where to start. As with most, this was likely the hardest thing to digest. I specifically struggled with accepting two main areas.

1. Not being able to lean on my own results

I have great results. I've worked hard to figure out and master a lot of strategies. I believe in everything I teach and its ability to help people. I want to be able to speak to the power of my education. Sure, I can talk about my results, but I have to be very careful, and I have to do it with a lot of context. Frankly, it's annoying. But the rules are the rules.

The good news is I'm doing it compliantly now and it works great. I'll get into why I like it even more below.

2. Not being able to use authentic, amazing testimonials

This one really hit me. I've worked hard to get great success stories. But establishing typicality is very difficult, and many times, out of our hands. If a customer is telling the truth and giving me a release, why can't I tell the world? Why am I not allowed to inspire people?

Well, I've accepted after a long time that a true business tracks their customers. A true business knows the experience and results of the typical customer. Forget the regulators for a minute. As business owners, it's our responsibility to make sure we are tracking our customers, and that they're experiencing success.

If they're not, it's not their problem; it's ours. We need to own it and fix it. Work hard enough at that and guess what? You can actually establish typical results, and use it in your marketing and have a leg up on all your competition. Not to mention, you'll have raving customers.

In the end, for me, the biggest difference that has made me into a believer is simple…

The types of customers we get when we use hype, crazy testimonials, claims, and un-founded promises are bad customers. They're coming in with the wrong expectations. They churn. They refund. They chargeback.

They drive your support team crazy. They write complaints. They fill Google with negative reviews.

These customers may give you money quickly, but they give you a whole lot of other things too. And in the end, we're to blame. We tell the customer they can have easy results in 30 days, and then we get upset with them for not putting in the work and for holding us responsible.

The side-benefit I've found from running a compliant marketing model is that I'm attracting amazing customers. These are lifelong customers who will spend many times more with me than the prior customers.

I can confidently say that we have stopped making claims and flipped the script. We speak specifically to how we can't make claims, and that they would be wrong and misleading. Our customers love and respect us for it, and they join us for the right reasons.

Surprisingly, the better the customers we attract, the more they apply what we teach and the closer we are to soon having an established typical result that we can use in our marketing—completely legally.

Chapter 15: Substantiation

Anik Singal

The Pentagon of Compliance

(1) MISREPRESENTATION
(2) NET IMPRESSION
(3) CLAIMS
(4) SUBSTANTIATION
(5) TESTIMONIALS
— COMPLIANCE

- Did you know that 72% of statistics are actually made up?
- Did you know that diabetes kills 3 times as many people per year as smoking?
- Did you know that I made $16.2 million in profit last year?

Did you also know that I just made all of that up? Yes, it was complete nonsense. Not one bullet point was true. But if I said it with conviction, and in any other context, you can see how people would believe me, right?

Don't Say That

Well, I have news for you. Not everything you hear on the internet is true, and as far as the FTC is concerned, they believe that most of what you hear in advertising is not true. The regulators have rightfully grown very skeptical.

By the way, this is not just about income claims. Plenty of advertisers use catch phrases to get customers to believe in their products. We hear these all the time:

- 4 out of 5 doctors recommend this…
- Dentist approved…
- The #1 voted truck…
- Tests prove this treatment works…
- Studies show this diet will help you lose weight…

There are many kinds of claims made all the time, and each and every one of them needs substantiation.

substantiation
[suhb-stan-shee-**ey**-shuhn] SHOW IPA
See synonyms for *substantiation* on Thesaurus.com

noun
1. evidence sufficient to establish a thing as true, valid, or real; proof:
   The department may require employees to provide vouchers, receipts, or other substantiation for any fees or expenses claimed.
2. the act or process of establishing or proving the truth of something:
   For scientific substantiation of health effects, the nutrients in these vitamin capsules must first be accurately measured.

Image Source: Dictionary.com[9]

---

[9] Dictionary.com. Substantiation definition.
https://www.dictionary.com/browse/substantiation.

Here is an example to show you how detailed the FTC can get when they are evaluating substantiation. In 2013, they brought a case against the Wellness Support Network for using the feedback of just one doctor to make a very strong claim about two products: a Diabetic Pack and Insulin Resistance Pack. They basically claimed that their products could treat, prevent, or cure diabetes and replace prescribed diabetes medication. This was of course a very strong claim.

More specifically, a claim the FTC quoted them on was "Diabetes Breakthrough" and a "clinically proven natural solution to diabetes with a 90% success rate."

It turns out, the doctor they quoted had made some general statements about the products offered by WSN, not the specific products in question. His research and studies were more related to the ingredients of the products, not the products themselves. Also, the FTC argued that the doctor never made a statement or substantiated any of the specific claims that the regulators were investigating.

5	2. Dr. Charles did not need to mention the subject claims in order to testify that the Defendants' products do what they say.
6	
7	In its Motion, at 7, FTC argues that Dr. Charles's testimony is irrelevant because his "two reports
8	never mention the claims challenged by the FTC." Consequently, FTC argues, Dr. Charles's reports "are
9	not helpful to the Court in determining the central issue in this case: whether the challenged claims are
10	truthful and substantiated." Motion, at 8. The FTC's argument misses the forest for the trees.

Image source: FTC (2013)[10]

It's clear in this case that, even when WSN attempted to substantiate their claims, the FTC went into the weeds on substantiation. WSN ended up having to settle with the FTC for $2.2 million because they failed to convince the FTC that they had proper substantiation for their claims.

---

[10] FTC. 2013. United States District Court Central District of California. Case No. 10-cv-04879-JCS. https://www.ftc.gov/system/files/documents/cases/131004wsnorder.pdf.

The bolder the claim, the more solid your substantiation needs to be, including proof such as:

- Studies
- Research
- Experts
- Repeated results
- Documentation
- Independent reviews

True substantiation in the FTC's eyes has no shortcuts and needs to be complete. If you think about it, there's a reason that it costs pharmaceutical companies billions of dollars to get a new medication approved. The amount of research and studies alone make up a majority of their expenses.

Here's a more light-hearted example from my case, but one that shows just how detailed the regulators get with substantiation.

Years ago, I won an award from BusinessWeek for being voted #2 Entrepreneur nationwide under the age of 25. I would mention this in my sales presentations as being in the "Top 3 Entrepreneurs under 25 as voted by BusinessWeek." Well, the FTC heard it and wanted to make sure I wasn't making it up.

The problem was that BusinessWeek no longer exists and all their webpages are gone, which is where they had published this story.

The FTC reached out and asked for proof. Now, I won this award over 15 years ago. Finding the physical magazines was nearly impossible. If we didn't find the substantiation, I could have been pinned for lying.

Luckily, arhives.org came to the rescue, and we found the article. To the same effect, once we substantiated that claim, they accepted it and removed it as one of their complaints against me. Substantiation works. If you have it, use it.

Absolute Statements

The level at which you have to provide substantiation depends on the claim being made. If you claim that something will cure diabetes, that's different from saying that your supplement can help increase your energy.

Absolute statements make definitive and unconditional claims that have absolutely zero room for exceptions. These statements usually make very confident and very specific claims. They're excellent in marketing, but lethal legally. Here are a few examples of absolute statements:

- **Guaranteed to Work**: This claim implies that the product will work for everyone, without exception. The advertiser needs to have evidence that the product is effective in "every case."
- **100% Safe**: Claiming a product is entirely safe is an absolute statement. The FTC would expect proof that the product poses absolutely no risk to any user in any circumstance.
- **Will Cure All Cases of ...**: This is a strong health-related claim that requires substantial clinical evidence showing that the product effectively treats every instance of the specified condition.
- **Lasts a Lifetime**: This claim implies that the product will never wear out or need replacement, which requires evidence of the product's durability and longevity over an indefinite period.
- **Stops All Engine Leaks**: This absolute claim suggests the product can fix every possible type of engine leak, which would require comprehensive evidence covering all scenarios.
- **Eliminates All Germs and Bacteria**: Such a statement implies complete effectiveness in killing germs and bacteria, which means you need thorough scientific testing and proof.
- **Never Fails**: This statement implies a zero-failure rate, which is a strong claim requiring robust supporting evidence.

You can see how each of these makes an absolute claim that has no room for conditions or deviation. If such is the case, the FTC will normally start their investigation there.

One case that was centered around absolute statements was against a company called POM Wonderful in 2013. They were accused of making strong absolute statements in the form of claims that they could cure or prevent heart disease, prostate cancer, and even erectile dysfunction. When arguing their case, the company said that pomegranates had been around for thousands of years and that everyone knew they had health benefits.

The FTC still demanded substantiation that their specific product could have the results they claimed. They demanded the company provide at least two unbiased clinical trials that backed up their claim. The company was not able to and immediately had to stop using all their claims.

Here are some examples of claims they made, taken directly from the FTC case summary:

- "You have to be on pomegranate juice. You have a 50 percent chance of getting [prostate cancer]. Listen to me. It is the one thing that will keep your PSA normal. You have to drink pomegranate juice. There is nothing else we know of that will keep your PSA in check. ... It's also 40 percent as effective as Viagra."
- Clinical studies prove that POM Juice and POMx prevent, reduce the risk of, and treat heart disease, including by decreasing arterial plaque, lowering blood pressure, and improving blood flow to the heart.

Again, the net impression from reading these would be that this product works for absolutely everyone. The "lack of conditions" makes them absolute statements and brings along the highest level of scrutiny.

General Statements

General statements are more broad and do not make specific and absolute claims. They use language that suggests a potential benefit without making concrete promises. Sometimes, marketers think they can "get around" the substantiation rules by adding words like "might" or "in some cases." But even if you're making your claims general, you still need substantiation. Remember, we discussed "implied claims" already, and this falls under that category.

Here are some examples of general statements:

- Our product is doctor recommended…
- Our parts exceed industry standards…
- Our smartwatch monitors heart rate accurately…

So what's wrong with these?

Well, who has recommended your product? Which doctor? Was it only one doctor? If so, that's a problem. If your parts exceed industry standards, how are you measuring that? Where's the proof? And if your smartwatch is accurate, where are the trials? Where's the data?

You can't just say something without having the studies to back it up, even if it's not quite as black and white as "our thing is the best."

I know it can be frustrating, but if you take a minute to look at it from the regulator's eyes, this makes sense. You need to have proof to back the things you say. It really comes down to common sense, and yes, this is me speaking as a marketer now, on the other side of the case.

How Do You Get Substantiation?

So, how do you get substantiation? Let's say you really do have the best training program in your niche. How can you prove what you're saying in a way that complies with the regulations? What qualifies as substantiation?

Using the examples we just talked about, here are some ways you can substantiate your claims.

For absolute claims:

- *Our investment returns beat every other fund*: You would have to have the data from literally every other fund in the world to make this claim. Better to just say, "Our investment returns outperform the national average." Use an easily verifiable standard. But even here, you need to know what the national average is, and you need to have uncontested documentation of your performance. In an ideal world, you should get a third-party company to review this and confirm your statement.
- *Our product uses a secret ingredient that no one else has*: There's no way to know if anyone else in the world has your specific ingredient. If you want to lean into the mystery, you can just say, "Our product uses a secret little-known ingredient..." You could substantiate this, but you would need to get all the products in your space, take them to a lab, break them down, and prove what their ingredients are. Instead, focus on what you have (that you can prove), and don't make statements about what someone else has or doesn't have.

For the more general statements, you could change it up like this:

- *Our product is doctor recommended*: The problem with this statement is that the customer will assume there has been some broader study, rather than just one or two doctors. If you truly do want to say it's doctor recommended, then commission a true study. Hire a third-party consulting firm. It'll be expensive, but it may open you up to being able to make this claim. We find it better to just stay more generic or even say "This product is recommended by Dr. XYZ, a Board Certified cardiologist with 20 years of experience. Here's what he said." I believe this carries the same weight and is easy for you to substantiate (as long as you didn't create an incentive for the doctor to endorse you or in any other way manipulate the endorsement). If it's authentic, you'll get the result you need from a marketing side, and you'll be compliant and honest.

- *Our parts exceed industry standards*: Here, you would need to prove exactly how your parts exceed industry standards. You would need studies. You would need multiple experts to confirm. You would need a factual and data driven basis to say this. It won't be easy. It'll be up to you to decide if the investment is worth it. However, you could say something like, "The industry standards for 10 years have been XYZ. Here's how we ventured to exceed the standards." Your statement is softer, and one that will be easier for you to reasonably substantiate.

- *Our smartwatch monitors heart rate very accurately*: Here you would need to point to a specific study or methodology that tested the accuracy of your heart rate monitor. You could point to that study and say, "In an independent study of five heart rate monitors, ours scored 95 out of 100."

Basically, don't make stuff up. Don't push the envelope, if it feels like you're fudging the truth, the FTC is going to see right through it. Anytime you bring up doctors or studies, you'll need the hard data to prove your case. If you don't have that hard data, find a way to advertise that's not misleading.

Lawyer's Perspective

Greg Christiansen

It's pretty simple. Even as kids, we are prone to saying things like "Oh yeah? Prove it."

Imagine what the world would look like if every company ran around saying anything they felt like saying. The regulations around substantiation, although sometimes burdensome, are common sense.

Ever seen an Apple commercial for an iPhone. Do you ever hear them say that it's the best phone in the World? Not at all.

However, ever seen a commercial for a Ford Pick-up truck that compares themselves to other trucks? Absolutely. But if you were to dig deeper, you'd see the major investment that Ford made to run independent studies that unequivocally substantiate their claim.

The same rules apply to big companies and smaller companies. The only reason we see the lack of substantiation more often in smaller businesses is that they skip the steps of doing the studies because they are expensive. Bigger companies generally have stricter legal compliance policies that catch that.

It's simple. If you say something, anything, make sure you have proof for it. Period.

Chapter 16: Testimonials

Greg Christiansen

The Pentagon of Compliance

1. MISREPRESENTATION
2. NET IMPRESSION
3. CLAIMS
4. SUBSTANTIATION
5. TESTIMONIALS

(Center: COMPLIANCE)

Testimonials are the low hanging fruit for regulatory bodies like the FTC when attacking marketing, particularly since 99.9% of marketers use them incorrectly. This is why testimonials tend to be the first thing the FTC looks at when starting an investigation against a company.

Pop quiz. You're a weight loss coach, you've had a lot of success, years in the industry, and tons of very happy customers. You've built an amazing Facebook community of very happy members. The main thing in the community is that people love posting their results. They post their before/after pictures to celebrate their wins and inspire others along their journey.

The community is vibrant and positive and very public.

One of your clients posts a superb celebration. They put their before picture and their after picture. The results are awesome. They also post all the details of when they started, their journey, the ups and downs, how much weight they lost, and exactly what parts of your training helped them.

The question is this, can you take a screenshot of the "testimonial" and use it in your marketing?

Think about it. It's got the before, the after, enough details to be substantiated; it even talks about the specific parts of your course that helped them. So, what's the answer? Can you use this testimonial?

The answer unfortunately is "no, not yet." In this chapter, I'll explain why it would be a violation to simply take a screenshot of the post and begin using it in your marketing, regardless of the appearance of substantiation.

So, why the focus on testimonials?

In the 1990s, celebrity endorsements were used a lot. Also, the use of quick disclosures, such as "results not typical, earnings may vary," became too wide. It got so bad that the FTC studied the situation and determined that the disclosures were mostly useless in the way they were being used.

In 2009, the FTC established its "Endorsement and Testimonials Guidelines in Advertising (16 CFR Part 255)." At this point, they put the world on notice that the old ways of disclosing statements and substantiation no longer applied.

Unfortunately, there are many companies that continue to use testimonials completely illegally because they completely ignore the Endorsement and Testimonial Guidelines. In fact, it is quite possible you have never heard of them before. The problem is that, for a period of time, there were many bad apple companies that were just making up flat out fake testimonials. And given that it became very difficult to decipher between real and fake, the FTC decided to just put strict rules in place for everyone.

One of the examples of this was Sage Auto Group, who, in 2016, were investigated for flat out using fake testimonials to sell their cars. They posted these testimonials, often ones they wrote themselves, all over social media and on rating sites like Yelp. It ended up costing them a $3.6 million settlement fine.

Here's a shot of the complaint describing the testimonial violation:

18	2. **Defendants Have Posted and Promoted Deceptive Consumer Testimonials and Endorsements.**
19	
20	Defendants deceptively have posted or promoted reviews appearing on third-party websites, like Facebook, Google+, and Yelp, that purport to be independent and objective but that are written by Defendants' employees, managers, and agents. These phony reviews—written by many of the same employees consumers are supposed to depend on during the sales and financing process—have sought to bolster Sage Auto's reputation and undermine the many negative reviews Defendants have received, including reviews that highlight their unlawful practices. *See* PX1 ¶¶ 50, 70-73 and Atts. CD-CI at 350-76, DY-EB at 537-47.
21	
22	
23	
24	
25	
26	
27	
28	For example, one sales representative purporting to be objective and

Image source: FTC (2016)[11]

---

[11] FTC. 2016. United States District Court Central District of California. Case No. 2:16-cv-07329-CAS(AJWx). https://www.ftc.gov/system/files/documents/cases/162006uc-nissan-memo.pdf.

Of course, "don't use fake testimonials" is an understandable offense. However, what if the testimonial isn't fake? What if it's real? There's a line of companies, including Lurn, that had real testimonials. However, using them was still a violation because the companies did not meet the following four-part criteria.

Here are the four rules that are mandatory if you want to use a specific "results-based" testimonial in your marketing.

Rule #1: Proper Release and Authorization
Make sure you have a proper release and authorization to use the testimonial, preferably with an affidavit confirming the truth and accuracy of the statement.

The customer needs to specifically sign a document and allow you to use their testimonial, picture, words, and story in your marketing. This may not sound like a big deal, but I have seen the worst from those who did not.

One of my clients got sued, not by the FTC, but by one of their own successful customers, who had given them a testimonial. The client ran a product launch and used a ton of testimonials in their launch. They had taken these truthfully right from their community.

At the end of the launch, they were congratulating each other in private, and ended up revealing that the launch had earned tens of millions of dollars. One of the women who had given a testimonial heard, and she found out that her testimonial, face, and likeness had been in all their marketing. Yet she had not given them written consent. So, she sued them for a portion of their revenue that she claimed was due to her story.

The regulators also require these releases. As a matter of fact, any time you use someone's name, picture, or experience in anything commercial, federal and state privacy laws require you have their written permission before using them.

Rule #2: Documentation to Support Claims (Substantiation)
There's that word again—substantiation. This is interesting though. Almost every marketer I speak to never considers this. Any results ever discussed by a client on a testimonial must be documented, substantiated, and privately verified by you or your team.

You can't just take their word for it.

You need to see contractual documents, bank accounts, transactions, and more. Here's how it works. When the customer mentions their results, it is their own claim. However, when you take those results and use them in your marketing, you have suddenly adopted that claim, and now it is your claim.

Hence, *you* need to substantiate it, not them.

Here's an example:

> "I bought this coaching program and within 5 months, I've made $32,000 flipping houses. I've done 7 deals and it was so easy. There's no way I could have done this without Steve's help."

Let's assume this is 100% true. Well, to substantiate the claim in the testimonial, you would need to do the following:

1. You would need to confirm that they did seven deals. You'd need to see the closing statements for every one of them.
2. You would need to see the bank transactions.

3. There is a claim of $32,000 profit. You would need to see all the expenses involved in the property, including any repairs. You would then calculate the profits yourself and confirm that $32,000 was correct.
4. You would need to take all these documents and proof and store them in your own systems for as long as you are using that testimonial.

You could do a survey of all of your customers to see if there's a general trend toward increased sales. Yes, it may be difficult to get a customer to give up all this private information. However, if you want to use the testimonial, the substantiation is an absolute requirement.

Rule #3: Typicality of Results
By far, the toughest of the rules is this one. I have to tell clients all the time. It doesn't matter if it's true. If it's not typical, it is a misrepresentation. Let's borrow the testimonial from above:

> "I bought this coaching program and within 5 months, I've made $32,000 flipping houses. I've done 7 deals and it was so easy. There's no way I could have done this without Steve's help."

Let's assume that you got the signed release. Let's also assume that you got all the substantiation. It's 100% true, you've cross-checked it all. Chances are you still can't use this testimonial "as is" because it doesn't meet the third rule of "typicality." This is exactly where most marketers fail, and this also happens to be the #1 focus of the FTC. Let me explain this, first from the eyes of a regulator.

Let's say you have 1,000 customers. Out of that, ten of them have gone on to have huge results. They applied what you taught, they may have had some business experience already, maybe even some other advantages.

Things hit for them, and each of them have had big results. Let's say each has made six figures. Obviously, as a marketer, you are going to want to use those ten stories, highlight them and focus on them.

Now, what is the "net impression" that's being created by these ten testimonials?

The net impression is that the average result of their customer is to make six figures, when in actuality, 90% of the 1,000 don't even take any action, so they make $0. Of the 100 who do something, 50 fail. Of the 50 who don't fail, 30 make $10,000 or less.

So, in essence, the "average customer" gets nowhere near the six figure "what's possible" testimonials you are using. Again, it all falls under the umbrella of net impression.

The regulators are very clear on this. You either only show testimonials of the typical result, or you don't show results-driven testimonials and stick to using generic character and experience testimonials only (which work great, by the way).

If you are going to use results-based testimonials, be sure they reflect a typical result. Remember substantiation. You need to be able to aptly prove your typical result claim.

Rule #4: Clear and Proximate Disclosures
This one is pretty easy, but most marketers do it wrong. Assuming you have met the first three requirements, the final one is the proper use of disclosures. Any disclosures related to the testimonial should be clear, prominent, and in close proximity to the claim they are qualifying.

It's not enough to just have one disclaimer somewhere at the beginning or end of your marketing messages, which is what most marketers do.

In Anik's case, even though he has many disclaimers all over the place, the FTC wasn't happy and questioned the placements many times. Each time you make a claim, you must be sure to have a disclaimer nearby and well blended in. If it's audio, you must make the disclaimer in an audio fashion. If it is a sales page, you must put the disclaimer in written words that are easy to see near the testimonial.

The crazy thing about disclosures and disclaimers is that using them doesn't protect you, but not using them hurts you. So, if you break the rules, but slap a disclaimer on, it won't help. You can not disclaim your way out of breaking the rules.

However, if you don't use a disclaimer, you can get penalized for that.

How Can I Use Testimonials?

If there is ever an area that my clients get the most frustrated, it's here. Learning that you can't use the amazing success stories of your customers is a big downer for marketers. However, if you change your systems, you can indeed use testimonials. I'll give you two options. Both work great.

Option #1: Character & Experience Testimonials Only—"Satisfaction Results"

My #1 recommendation to clients is to not use specific results-driven testimonials, especially monetary ones. Use general testimonials, where the customer is discussing the amazing training, the community, the guidance, and their satisfaction and excitement.

Although you still need the signed release, you will not have anything to substantiate. Before you question it, ask Anik. These work very well, and you'll be surprised at how well they still keep your conversions high but remove a lion's share of regulatory risk.

Granted, these work best for presentations to warm audiences. So, if you're marketing aggressively and scaling to cold audiences and need to use results-based testimonials, then do what Beach Body does.

Option #2: Get Typical Results Data
Beachbody does an amazing job with this. Let's take their P90X program. When you buy the program, before you can even sign-in, you have to sign an agreement. Guess what's in the agreement? A release.

Rule #1, satisfied.

Now, BeachBody has created a members area that is very engaging and interactive. Not only does it help BeachBody legally, but it gives customers an amazing experience. In order to start the training, the company asks you to upload your before picture.

They ask you to subsequently check-in throughout the P90X program, upload pictures weekly, update logs, leave notes, participate in the community, and much more. What are you accomplishing by doing this? You're creating substantiation and proof of your journey and results.

But also, you, as a customer, love the accountability and the occasional check-in by the company to see how you're doing.

Rule #2, satisfied.

Next, because BeachBody has this data on most of their customers, they're automatically building the typicality of results. What the company can do now is track and get specific data on what percent of their customers do the program and complete the program and what results they get at the end.

Now, the company can take all this data and create a statement around which they can show testimonials:

> "For the average customer who enrolled in P90X, finished it completely and followed the exercise and diet plan for 90 days, they saw an average weight loss of ten pounds."

Notice how they're not going to say, "Our average customer loses ten pounds." They're being specific to say that this is the typical result of someone who finishes the program and they have all the data and proof to back it up. Now, because of the unique way the training is being delivered...

Rule #3, satisfied.

And finally, every time they show a testimonial, they'll make sure there's an easily visible disclaimer reminding the prospects that the program has to be completed exactly and fully, and even then, the results are not guaranteed.

Rule #4, satisfied.

You can use testimonials, but you have to decide how much work you want to put into the process of substantiating them. If your product is truly excellent and it gets results from your customers, take a little time to copy BeachBody, and you will get a competitive marketing advantage that is completely legal.

Marketer's Perspective
Anik Singal

Yes, I get it. It's tough. It even sucks a little bit. But hey, it is what it is.

Good news. I'm doing a ton of marketing and using social proof (like pictures of happy customers with my product) and general character or experience testimonials. I was convinced these would flop and my conversions would plummet. But even on paid ads to cold audiences, these testimonials are doing great.

Adapting these new testimonial rules was one of the hardest marketing shifts I've ever made, but I'm glad I did and I'm far happier with my marketing and the results now than I've ever been. Not to mention, I'm far happier with the quality of customers I'm getting.

So, before you knock it, try it.

Anyways, it's not like you have a choice.

Chapter 17: Goal-Setting

Greg Christiansen

It is my professional opinion that Anik's case truly came down to just four words that were said on his sales calls. It is crazy to think that so much of his two decades of hard work and the bright future of the company hinged on these four words.

Also, my experience shows that most attorneys don't even know about the harm these four words can create. The four words center around an unspoken rule called "goal setting." Basically, in private meetings, the FTC leadership has said that "goal setting" is a form of implied earnings claims. Unfortunately, there is no public documentation on it, but I can tell you without a shadow of doubt that this is one of the most scrutinized rules.

So, what were the four words?

"What is your goal?"

Seems pretty harmless to ask someone this. At least, that's what most people think. I'll tell you that this question has been in almost every sales script I have ever reviewed. It's being taught by the top sales trainers. They call it future pacing, and it has become a common practice.

Well, as it turns out, the FTC doesn't like it, at all.

When Anik was early in his investigation, he was convinced that his sales calls were completely compliant. After all, he'd spent a lot of money in legal review, he had a full-time paralegal on staff just to review the calls, and he took call compliance very seriously. He'd even created some very thorough review processes and scoring systems.

He was convinced that after getting an independent third-party review, he would be able to convince the FTC that the calls are not problematic in the eyes of the law. So, he asked my firm to do the call reviews. Keep in mind that, at this time, I was not representing Anik as his attorney. Given everything he had told me, I felt there was a good chance these calls would be compliant.

Five calls in, I was sitting in my vacation cabin dreading having to call Anik. Yes, the calls were compliant in the eyes of what he knew to be compliant. The calls were actually very good. However, I had immediately identified the issue only five calls in.

Goal setting.

Some of the first calls I heard had the question, "What is your goal?"

It was clear that Anik had no intention of breaking the law, but this was one that he just didn't know about. The only reason I know about this unspoken rule is because I have been physically in the FTC offices and heard the leadership at the commission specifically state:

> "Do you set goals with your clients? Yes? Then that's implied earnings claims and you're violating the law."

Although Anik ran a stand-up operation, I had to deliver to him the bad news and my prediction of where I felt the FTC would eventually focus their investigation. Months later, it turned out I was correct. The case came down solely to the $14 million Lurn had processed using telesales. And the goal setting became the central non-compliance issue.

The Commission's stance on this is that asking this question is a leading question. You are future-pacing the client, and when the client answers and you agree with their answer, you are giving them the "net impression" that they can easily attain those results.

You are committing to a result on behalf of the client that you have no substantiation or typicality study to backup.

> 60. Lurn's telemarketers follow scripts to sell the consulting programs, and the scripts are consistent between the programs. Telemarketers are instructed to ask consumers about their current income, how much they would like to make, and how the increased income would affect the consumers' lives.
>
> 61. After the initial interview, the script directs the telemarketers to say "I'm 100% confident we can help you" get the results that the consumers wish for. The telemarketers are instructed to confirm that consumers can achieve the desired earnings regardless of the program, the consumer's experience, or the amount of money the consumer hopes to attain.
>
> 62. Consumers have frequently told Lurn's telemarketers that they hope to earn six figures a year or enough to provide a full-time income. Lurn's telemarketers have routinely assured consumers they are 100% confident that Lurn can help the consumers get there.

Image Source: FTC (2023)[12]

Now, in the defense of Anik, he says that the "we're 100% confident" was not nearly as pervasive throughout the calls as the FTC is stating. In these types of settlements, there will always be disagreements. However, the

---

[12] FTC. 2023. United States District Court for the District of Maryland. https://www.ftc.gov/system/files/ftc_gov/pdf/FiledLurnComplaint.pdf.

FTC does have the right to write the complaint letters as they want, and you typically have no ability to change them.

Having said that, whether the "100% confident" line was there or not, the line of questioning the sales agents took, for the most part, was not compliant.

You'll notice that the Commission doesn't use the words "goal setting," but trust me when I say, I've had countless direct conversations with them where this term is common and used consistently. The question about goals on a phone call is downright dangerous and immediately turns the entire call into a compliance time bomb.

Now, if the customer ends up stating a goal on their own without being asked, fine. But the responsibility is still on the sales agent to go out of their way to correct the customer and assure them that there are no guarantees and that they are only there to be an educational resource.

Unfortunately, "not knowing" is not a defense with the regulators. Had Anik and I worked together before, I would have absolutely told him to remove that question from the script, and I know he would have. If they'd taken out the "goal setting," we would have had a defensible position with the FTC. While I would have gone to battle with the FTC over the issue, if necessary, I knew the goal setting was a weak spot in our position. Unfortunately, sometimes it only takes one issue.

I bet only a dozen attorneys in America understand "goal setting" in telemarketing calls. I only know it because I have invested twenty years now, with an emphasis in the FTC and State laws.

No matter what you're doing, check your sales scripts right now.

If you find this question in there, take it out immediately and thank Anik and I later.

Marketer's Perspective

Anik Singal

With all due respect, this one really irks me, and I holistically disagree with the stance of the FTC. To be clear, I disagree, but moving forward I will, of course, comply. I don't believe asking someone about their goals is a bad practice. I don't believe that giving a customer hope or believing in someone should be punished.

Now, I accept that if some of my agents had used the "100% confident" term, that's a problem. I hold my ground that it wasn't nearly as bad as it was made to seem in their letter, but history is history.

When it comes to asking someone about and validating their goals and offering to help them with those goals, I really hope the FTC changes their views on this. I understand there are marketers who violate this in a horrible way. I understand there are outright scams. I think there should be differentiation in how it's applied.

To think in my mind that my entire life, my company, everything I'd worked for, and even the fact that I was about to be acquired, was all lost due to just these four words. It's very difficult to digest, but let it be a lesson for you.

Yet I think the bigger lesson here is that, in the end, it can be just one thing you're doing that gets you in trouble. I cannot stress how important it is for you to understand the law and the rules and to make sure your legal representation does too.

And by the way, I mean you. This is not an issue to hand off (without monitoring) to your team, your business partner, or your COO.

I mean you.

Because, regulatory risk is something that can take away everything you've worked for with the snap of a finger. That's important enough that, no matter what your expertise or skills are, if you're the founder, you need to own compliance directly.

Chapter 18:
Selectivity, Qualification, & Scarcity

Greg Christiansen

It's 8 pm...

You're starting a webinar...

You've got hundreds of guests on...

They're excited. It's going to be an amazing night...

> *"Listen, I'm telling you right now that most of you won't even qualify for the offer today, but let's see. Just sit back and take notes and I hope you qualify to work with us..."*

And just like that, by 8:05 PM, the entire webinar has already become non-compliant. Because you just did a fake qualification. Be honest with me for a minute. What criteria are you really using to see if they qualify?

First, they're on a webinar and can buy on their own without anyone confirming their qualification. Second, the statement is being used mostly to create mystique.

Most of the time the only qualifications are:

1. They can breathe.
2. They can pay you money.

Well, these aren't qualifications, and every marketer in the world knows it.

The only reason you say that in the beginning is to create the "illusion" of something very special, an "insiders club" that people are privileged to get an invitation to. Well, this is a misrepresentation.

This has become an area that the FTC is really starting to enforce, especially when it comes to telesales calls, because it's being way overdone. I see fake qualification claims being made on VSLs, webinars, and telesales calls practically everyday. Some of them are innocent, but illegal nonetheless.

False Scarcity

False scarcity is a marketer's dream, and most marketers I know are using it. It taps into a customer's fear of missing out. We all know that if we can get people to stop thinking about pros and cons, and just go with their gut, they'll be more likely to buy quickly.

Have you ever heard of or used any of these techniques?

- Only 30 spots left.
- This price expires tonight.
- You'll never see this offer again.
- Limited time bonus.
- This bonus is for the first 100 customers only.

If I had to guess, I would say that a vast majority of the webinars I review have false scarcity in them.

These are all absolutely fine, if you can prove they are true without a shadow of doubt. If there are really only 30 spots left, and you keep record of the fact that you stopped selling at 30 spots, you're allowed to say it. However, I've never seen a claim like this made that was both true and had the proper substantiation. If you think about it, false scarcity is pretty much lying. If you say something to make a consumer think they have to rush to make a decision, in the eyes of the regulators, that's deception.

The FTC released a report where they classified false scarcity as a "dark pattern." The FTC says that dark patterns are "design(ed) practices that trick or manipulate users into making decisions they would not otherwise have made and that may cause harm."

SCARCITY	False Low Stock Message	Creating pressure to buy immediately by saying inventory is low when it isn't *Example: "Only 1 left in stock – order soon"*
	False High Demand Message	Creating pressure to buy immediately by saying demand is high when it isn't *Example: "20 other shoppers have this item in their cart"*
URGENCY	Baseless Countdown Timer	Creating pressure to buy immediately by showing a fake countdown clock that just goes away or resets when it times out *Example: "Offer ends in 00:59:48"*
	False Limited Time Message	Creating pressure to buy immediately by saying the offer is good only for a limited time or that the deal ends soon – but without a deadline or with a meaningless deadline that just resets when reached
	False Discount Claims	Creating pressure to buy immediately by offering a fake "discounted" or "sale" price

Image Source: FTC (2022)[13]

---

[13] FTC. 2022. Bringing Dark Patterns to Light. https://www.ftc.gov/system/files/ftc_gov/pdf/P214800%20Dark%20Patterns%20Report%209.14.2022%20-%20FINAL.pdf.

You can encourage a customer to make a decision, but you can't lie about urgency, pricing, units left, or any other metric that falsely rushes them into making the buying decision.

Fake Qualification

Fake qualifications are centered around a fictional or over exaggerated "selection process." If there are real qualifications, that's one thing. Maybe you're operating a legal services program and the people you invite have to be lawyers. That's a real qualification, and in that case, it's okay to transparently lay that out.

However, usually, "qualifications" are just being used to determine whether a customer has money or to create the aura of being "the chosen one," so you can increase conversions.

The FTC will look at it as deceptive, which it is. If there aren't real qualifications beyond just being a warm body, don't do this.

Here is an example where qualifications (or lack thereof) became the anchor of an FTC case—FTC vs Nudge, LLC, filed in 2020. In this case, the FTC and State of Utah clearly state that they feel the personal questions being asked of the prospects were for no real purpose:

> 160. The Nudge Defendants' telemarketers had access to the forms that consumers filled out at the Workshops detailing their personal finances. The Nudge Defendants' telemarketers also used scripts that instructed them to ask about the consumers' personal financial situation, including their credit card limits and savings.
>
> 161. In numerous instances, the Nudge Defendants' telemarketers tell consumers that they will use this personal financial information to assess whether the consumer would be an appropriate candidate for the program.
>
> 162. The Nudge Defendants' representations about how they use consumers' financial information are false.
>
> 163. The Nudge Defendants' telemarketers do not use this information to assess a consumer's qualifications for the program. Instead, the Nudge Defendants use this information to decide how much to charge consumers for the one-on-one coaching program. The Nudge Defendants charge consumers several thousand dollars, and as much as $20,000, to enroll in this program. The Nudge Defendants' telemarketers had discretion to set the cost of the program based in part on what the consumers had available in terms of credit and assets.

Image Source: FTC (2020)[14]

Personally, I was involved in this case, and I disagree with the FTC. Nudge, LLC, was selling a program that teaches their students how to invest in real estate. In order to do this, the student needed to have the appropriate financial resources.

The questions about their finances were very relevant. However, this became the anchoring issue. I'm seeing this become a central issue more and more, especially in telesales operations, where customers consistently fill out forms before the call.

---

[14] FTC. 2020. United States District Court District of Utah, Central Division. Case No. 2:19-cv-00867-DBB-DAO. https://www.ftc.gov/system/files/ftc_gov/pdf/1823016-nudge-first-amended-complaint_-_redacted.pdf.

Make sure you have a true purpose for the information you ask for, or you will fall into this false qualification trap.

Qualifying Related Red Flags

Here are some other red flags that the FTC and other government bodies look for:

- Focusing too much on how much someone earns (unless it's truly directly relevant).
- Focusing on how much someone has in savings (again, unless it's truly relevant).
- Asking for someone's credit score.
- Asking whether they're a homeowner or not.

These are all red flags because the regulatory bodies say you're just asking this to gauge how much money someone has, so you can sell them. So, if your "qualifications" include any of those red flags, cut them out, unless they're truly required for your product or service.

That brings us to true qualifications. What if you truthfully have a minimum income requirement, net worth requirement, credit score requirement, or professional experience requirement?

If your qualification statements are true, then they're true. But you need to adequately document it. You need a record of everyone who has been turned away, and it needs to be a respectable volume of people. As long as you have these records and can confirm you're following your own rules, you can use these qualifying statements. However, if you're always making exceptions and have many customers who get in who do not meet those requirements, you're walking into trouble.

Marketer's Perspective

Anik Singal

We all know that exclusivity and scarcity sells, but if you're making it up, let's face it, you're just lying. Marketers convince themselves that it's an innocent fib and nobody's getting hurt. However, you've misrepresented the facts, created a different net impression, and rushed someone into making a monetary decision.

If you were on the other side, you wouldn't like it. This is exactly why the governing bodies are putting an emphasis on this. I've completely removed the word "qualify" and any form of urgency or scarcity from all my marketing. My conversions are great, unaffected, and I keep my integrity with my customers.

It turns out that for the right customer and to build a business full of value, you don't need false qualifiers and scarcity. Trust me, just try it.

Chapter 19:
Refunds & Guarantees

Greg Christiansen

Do you have a refund policy? Do you honor it? Do you make it hard for your customers to get a refund? Or have you just flat out created a "no refunds policy"?

How do you think a customer feels when they truly want a refund and don't get it? Although some may say, "terms are terms," many do not leave it at that. When they don't get a refund directly from the company, they seek other ways, such as:

- Leaving negative reviews about you online
- Complaining to the BBB (which goes into the Sentinel system)
- Writing their State A.G. about you (which goes into the Sentinel system)
- Suing you (which the regulatory bodies can see)
- Issuing class action lawsuits (prime area for regulators to hang out)

Ultimately, all these things get you into a regulator's path and leave you with a much bigger issue than a $1,000 refund request.

In Anik's case, one of the main requests from the FTC was that they wanted to see every single refund request in three years, and also his response to each one. What do you think they were looking for? They wanted to see how Lurn treated its customers, and how they protected the customers when needed. No "saved sale" is worth the headache it can cause you, whether it be negative publicity online or being reported to a variety of consumer protection regulators.

It's certainly not worth it when you realize that rejecting refunds is one of the easiest ways to get investigated by the FTC. Just refund the customers who aren't happy. Period. And if that means your refund rate is through the roof, then let's be honest, you have a bigger problem on your hands that you need to fix.

Initially, marketers had liberal refund policies, then they realized their refund rate was too high. Many decided to go to a "no refund policy" and realized that isn't fully legal, either. Now, marketers have another trend going on, and they're starting to get tricky.

Marketers are now doings a couple of different things, which are:

- Asking for signed waivers of no refunds
- Creating a barrage of conditions to "qualify" for a refund

If there's anything worse than not refunding, it's looking like you have a refund policy, but then misleading or tricking a customer and not honoring it. The regulators hate that even more. If you want to do conditional refunds, you have to go out of your way to make sure that you're very clear about the conditions before the sale.

Regardless, my advice to clients typically is, even if the client doesn't qualify per your terms, issue the refund.

Special Class of Customers To Refund Even Faster

Your refund policy should be liberal with all customers, but there are some groups you need to be extra sensitive to. This is because regulators protect them even more aggressively, and they have their own agencies that protect them over and above the protection offered by the State Attorney General or FTC. These groups include:

- Seniors
- Disabled people
- Veterans

If you think about it, it makes sense. These are people that are less able to protect themselves and are more vulnerable to being tricked or manipulated. However, be careful because you're not allowed to decline customers because of their age or health. That's blatant discrimination.

You absolutely need to be aware and vigilant and make sure you are ready to refund them in case of any issues. I cannot stress this enough.

Thankfully, in Anik's case, he always treated his customers with great respect. The FTC inquired about their refunds and support requests. After he submitted all his documents, that was the last we heard about it. One can only assume there was nothing there. Did this alone protect him from being investigated? No. Did this help him in the settlement and reduce the injunctions and future bans?

Absolutely.

A Refund Period is MANDATORY—Cooling Off Period

Notice that above I said that many companies decide to have a "no refund policy" all together. The term I see most often is "all sales are final." But what about the state or federal "Cooling Off" Period?

Each state has their own rules that they put under "Rights to Rescission," and the FTC issued a rule called "Cooling Off Rule."

Don't Say That

> **16 CFR Part 429**
>
> **Rule Summary:**
> The Cooling Off Rule provides that it is unfair and deceptive for sellers engaged in "door-to-door" sales valued at more than $25 to fail to provide consumers with disclosures regarding their right to cancel the sales contract within three business days of the transaction.

Image Source: FTC[15]

Basically, if you're selling anything online that costs over $25, you are legally required to have a cooling-off period (aka. refund period) of three days from the date of purchase. This especially applies to coaching programs.

Not only is it required that you have this refund period, but here's some other things to know about it:

- It's absolute. No exceptions.
- It's unconditional. They can request it for any reason.
- It's required that the seller inform the customer about the cooling-off period. You can't hide it. This means it needs to be prominent on their contract and receipt, so they know.

I cannot begin to tell you how many clients I have who are completely unaware of this rule. They're violating it daily. I can also tell you that outside of the FTC, I have had to defend multiple clients against class-action or consumer lawsuits in regards to not being informed about the cooling-off period.

The problem is that the regulators say, if you didn't inform the customer, it essentially means you have an infinite refund policy for any customer. Any of them can ask for a refund at any time and you're legally required to issue it.

---

[15] FTC. Cooling-off Period for Sales Made at Home or Other Locations. https://www.ftc.gov/legal-library/browse/rules/cooling-period-sales-made-home-or-other-locations.

The next thing to be aware of is that each state has their own rules. Some states have a cooling-off period that is more than three days. Customers in those states need to be issued a refund as per the laws of that state, or you're open to being sued by the state Attorney General or a class action attorney.

Here are some examples:

- Alaska: Up to 15 days, depending on the type of sale.
- California: Up to 7 days, depending on the product sold.
- Florida: As high as 30 days for limited types of products.
- Utah: Up to 5 days.

You need to inquire about the state you do most of your business in.

Marketer's Perspective
Anik Singal

No matter what the government or anyone else says, I stand by the team and company we built. We had an immaculate customer experience, and we obsessed over our customers. I'm proud of the fact that, even though the FTC had issues with other areas of our marketing, our customer treatment, refunds, and support teams were never brought into question.

However, this didn't come easy. We worked very hard to make sure our customers were happy, as follows:

- Our average support response time was 36 minutes.
- We had three support teams worldwide, working 8-hour shifts.
- Our refund rate was less than 5%.
- Our chargeback rate was near .7%.
- BBB was an A Rating.

So, how did we manage to do all this while still having a liberal refund policy? With:

- Clear sales messaging to deter "looky-loos."
- An amazing customer support team, so everyone got replies fast.
- Calling customers who were stuck.
- Excellent products and delivering what we promised.

It is absolutely possible to have 60,000+ transactions in three years and still have an amazing refund rate and customer experience. But it also meant that, in our company, our support and operations team was one of our largest teams.

I poured millions into that team. I remain proud of it and will do it in every company I ever build. I recommend you do the same. Customers first. Always.

Chapter 20:
Value Stacking

Greg Christiansen

Have you ever said this?

> "Act today and you get this entire online digital course, a total value of $38,760, for just $497, and you can begin changing your life instantly."

Okay, let's pause.

Seriously?

Are you telling me that your online course full of PDFs and videos is worth more than a brand new Tesla? Are you telling me that you're just so benevolent that you're giving away a $38,000 course for $500?

You see where I am going with this, right? Well, so does the FTC. Honestly, sometimes, if you step back and just look at the things marketers and advertisers do, you can see how dishonest some of it appears. You can't put a value on your course that is not based on reality. And you can't offer it at a ridiculous discount and expect the FTC not to raise their eyebrows.

So, what is the RULE?

Simple. Substantiate it.

If you want to say something is worth $1,000, you need to have sold it at that. And not just two sales to your grandmother and best friend. You need to have legitimately sold a representative volume. This volume will be relevant to your business. The more transactions you get per year in total, the higher the number is to make your value representable.

One more thing, in order to give something an official value, you have to have sold that very product (not a variation or similar). A true value has to be established for that course. If you mark the value based off of something similar, there's a different way to approach it, which we'll discuss below.

Example:

You sell a product called ABC for $1,000. You've sold 150 units. ABC is worth $1,000.
But then you go and create XYZ. It's the same content as ABC but not the exact same course. Well, XYZ is not worth $1,000. The rules are the product and offering have to be the same.

In order to do a value or bonus stack, you need to make sure that each and every part of that stack is substantiated and sold previously at that price. Even then, I always ask my clients to be real. Saying something is valued at $38,000+ and is now selling for only $500. Just imagine how that sounds. Ask yourself what kind of customers it attracts? Even in cases where it may be substantiated, I encourage my clients to pick some more realistic figures.

Comparison Selling

Years ago, marketers did what marketers do best; found a way to bend the rules. When the regulators started making their opinions on "value stacking" clear, marketers decided to not use specific numbers, but start using "relative comparisons."

> "Finish our program in 1 week versus getting an MBA from Harvard, which will take 2 years! You can make an unlimited income with our program and a Harvard MBA will barely get you six figures and put you in debt for over $100,000."

I took this pretty much verbatim from a client's webinar. The issue here is multifold:

- **Misrepresentation**: Because the comparison is truly not apples-to-apples.
- **Lack of Substantiation**: You better have a typical result that beats an MBA graduate to get even close to saying this.
- **Net Impression**: People hold graduate degrees in high esteem. You're linking your program to the credibility behind an MBA. You're creating a net impression of big potential earnings and MBA-level credibility. This will not fly.

Also, I can tell you from personal experience that the leadership at the FTC holds traditional education in high-regard. Collegiate degrees, especially from esteemed Universities, are respected and promoted. Comparing yourself to that is just adding one more layer to your problems.

So, in summary...

When it comes to value stacking and comparison selling, just follow one simple rule. Stand back and look at it. Does it sound truly legitimate to you? Does it even sound real? If it doesn't, you have two problems.

1. You're attracting the attention of the FTC and other regulating bodies.
2. You're bringing in absolutely the wrong kind of customer. They'll complain, they'll demand a refund, and they won't come back.

Following the rules is not only good for compliance, it just brings you a better customer and builds a better business.

Marketer's Perspective

Anik Singal

Well.

This is a perfect example of bad habits being passed down from generation to generation in the marketing world. I used to sell packages worth $10,000. Then my competition created one worth $15,000, so I created one worth $20,000. Then they went to $25,000, and I went to $30,000, and so on.

The question is how are we truly valuing our bonuses? Unfortunately, "in the eye of the beholder" is not substantiation enough. For those of you who think this is not a big deal, I want to show you a clip right from my own Lurn FTC complaint letter.

Deceptive Marketing of the Email Startup Incubator Program

22. Defendants' Email Startup Incubator purports to teach consumers how to make substantial income through e-mail advertising and affiliate marketing. Email Startup Incubator costs $1,995, though Defendants claim the course offers over $37,710 of value.

Image Source: FTC (2023)[16]

---

[16] FTC. 2023. United States District Court for the District of Maryland. https://www.ftc.gov/system/files/ftc_gov/pdf/FiledLurnComplaint.pdf.

I offer no judgment, because even though I meant well, I never realized that the stacks were getting a bit out of hand. I found myself and my company going with the flow, and in the absence of my micro-managing oversight, the team continued the same trend I had started.

The good news is this.

I stopped. I don't add random values unless I have sold it at that price in the past. Guess what? It works just fine. No one cares. Actually, I do the opposite. I make fun of the fact that someone out there may value a PDF at $997. I just say, "Look, here's what I'm offering. It'll take you this much time and effort to learn on your own. You can attach whatever value you want to this. I think it's invaluable and will make your journey far easier."

These are all things that I believe to be true. All things that are clearly my opinion. All things that are converting just fine.

Chapter 21:
Key Phrases To Avoid

Greg Christiansen

My wife can't stand watching TV or movies with me anymore. I can't contain the lawyer within. We'll be watching TV and the commercials will come on. All of a sudden she'll hear me shout, "That's not true!"

She'll tell me to, "Be quiet and stop interrupting. Just watch the show."

But I can't help myself. "Did you hear them?" I'll argue. "They just said 'risk-free.' Nothing is risk free! Are they going to compensate me for missed opportunities, time spent, and any losses incurred? Just because they give me my original money back, doesn't make it risk-free!"

And just like that, I know I have been hanging around lawyers from the FTC for too long.

If you think about it, we're surrounded by advertising that is just littered with problematic words. I'm not saying that using any of these words will automatically get you sued by the FTC, but these are the very words that end up creating a bad "net impression."

Largely as a habit and practice, I ask my clients to start eliminating these words from their marketing. Of course, you can still use them, but it all depends on the context. The reason I list them here is because I feel that the majority of the time I see marketers using them, they are creating problems.

This is not a complete list, but one that should give you a good idea of what to look for:

- **Easy**: *"So easy, a child could do this…"*
- **Step-by-Step**: *"Don't worry, we give you one baby step at a time."*
- **Handholding**: *"We'll hold your hands every step of the way."*
- **Risk Free**: *"There is no risk to this!"*
- **No experience needed**: *"Anyone can do it, 100% no experience needed."*
- **Guaranteed**: *"This is guaranteed to work."*
- **Completely automated**: *(100% Done for you)*
- *You can do this in your sleep…*
- *100% passive income.*
- *It takes just one click…*
- *Use none of your own money (OPM)*

So what is the problem with these phrases? Let's take a look.

So easy, a child could do it
When someone sees an ad that says a program is "easy" or "so easy a child could do it," think about the net impression you are creating. "So easy a child can do it" is telling someone that they're virtually guaranteed to succeed.

A child can't do much, so they won't have to do much. But the truth is that, in almost any field, the customer will have to learn things. They'll have to try things. They'll hit obstacles. They'll face struggles, failures, and even some losses.

The customer is going to have to use their brain and really strive through the challenges. None of this sounds like something you would expect a child to do.

When I ask my clients about this and really drive the point home, most of them immediately say "You're right. We should take that out." The reason is because, even if innocent, it's clearly a false statement.

And, it severely impacts the net impression you're creating (in a bad way).

Step-by-step
"Buying real estate is easy with us. We've laid out the entire plan for you step by step. You don't even have to think. Just do what we tell you."

Do you see why context matters? It's not that the words "step by step" are a problem. However, when they're used in a way to make someone believe that they don't have to even think, well, ask yourself what that is doing to the net impression? If you do have a step by step program, you can say this, but also layer in some context, such as, "You still have to learn and do the work, but we've tried to break it down as much as we can."

Hand-holding
"We hold your hand the entire way. You'll never feel alone."

I've been a compliance attorney to marketers for two decades. I can say without a shadow of doubt that not one offer I've reviewed truly offers hand-holding the way they lead a consumer to believe. Unless you're letting your customer move into your house and be with you 24/7, it's obviously illegal to lead them to think that.

"Hand-holding" is one of those terms I ask clients to permanently remove. I don't see how, even with context, you could use this term in an honest fashion. Ask yourself what a potential customer hears when they hear the term?

Don't Say That

The net impression is that there's nothing for them to do. They just have to show up and the results will be created by you and your "hand holding."

Strike this term from your marketing.

Risk-free
Nothing is risk-free. Even the drive from your house to your office isn't risk-free. The walk up the stairs to your bedroom isn't risk-free. The attorney in me absolutely cringes at this term. If you want to use this term, make it more specific.

"Your purchase price is risk-free."

The FTC is always worried that the underlying product you are offering seems to be "risk-free." Because in their eyes there is always a risk. When you're making a generic claim of "risk-free," you're helping the customer skip over or not think about all the other investments they're making:

- What about their time?
- What about other money they may invest?
- What about any potential losses (other than their purchase price)?
- What about opportunity cost? They could be doing other things than your course.

Even if the risk is small, there is risk. Period.

"Almost no risk" is also frowned upon. In the complaint letter against Lurn, here is an exact quote, "...*also claims to have a "tested proven system[,]" a business model with "almost zero risk[,]" and boasts that...*"

See how they hear it?

Anik and his team had a very strong justification as to why they said "almost zero risk." Honestly, it was about as close as I have personally ever come to agreeing with the claim. However, the FTC was absolutely not interested.

The idea of something being risk-free or minimal risk is repulsive and a big red flag for them.

No experience needed
Everything requires some level of experience. If you want to build an online business, you need to be able to use a computer, the Internet, online tools, and the English language. These may not be things that register as experience, but the regulators argue that it is.

Again, it comes down to net impression. When you tell someone, "anyone can do it, you don't need any experience" what they're hearing is "this is so easy, I can do it quickly!"

Again, most things being sold that the regulators are interested in are never that easy, such as:

- Building a business
- Investing money
- Flipping real estate

These are innately things that need some level of experience. The problem with this is, in my experience, very few individuals are able to pick up new concepts super fast. The use of the term "no experience" needed creates an implication that you can do this with only a few hours a week.

Most clients will find that, while they don't have experience in the particular industry or investment strategy you are advertising, they will need help and resources. If the use of "no experience" makes it appear to be too easy, you have misled them. I hate repeating myself but just read what you write and ask yourself, "What net impression am I creating?"

Guaranteed
What is guaranteed? The results someone gets? Well, need I say more?

You can never guarantee something that you can't control. So, again, unless you're letting your customer live in your home, and you'll practically do it for them, how can you guarantee results? Believe it or not, I see this far too many times, and it's a major red flag.

The other guarantee I see is a "money back guarantee."

Yet when the customer asks for a refund, it takes three days to get a response and the response is usually a series of questions. Then the company says, "Let's set up a phone call." Then the company says, "Please send us your original receipt." Then the company says, "We noticed you never logged in. You don't qualify." Then the company says, "How about we give you credit?" Then the company doesn't reply for seven days.

You may be laughing, but I see this a lot. What kind of a guarantee is it if the customer has to fight tooth and nail to get their money back. The truth is that it's not a guarantee; it's a nuisance. It's a misrepresentation.

If you make your refunds very easy, say it. If you don't, don't say it. But no matter what happens, don't even imply that you guarantee results.

Completely automated (100% Done for You)
The problem with this kind of absolute statement is it's the same as "risk-free" or "just one click." Nothing is completely automated. Even in the

case of services that are done for you, the client will always need to be involved. There'll be meetings, questions, services to buy, things to learn, decisions to be made.

Saying something is "completely automated" is just not true. Just like almost nothing is 100% passive, nothing is completely automated.

"Done for you" is another problem. Unless you're an agency, it's hard to use this term and not be misrepresenting. My main advice to clients is to steer away from it.

You can do this in your sleep…
This one is just a flat out lie. Why are we even saying this? I understand the intention the marketer has is to say, "The business is still running when you're asleep." Then, say that. However, saying that something is so easy that you can do it in your sleep has the worst net impression you can imagine.

"Once the business is up and running, your ads will continue to run, even at night. You will wake up to sales that have happened while you slept. This business has no hours of operation and never closes."

How much better is that? It's factually correct, but it also isn't setting up a crazy net impression. I would go even further to add context that the business still needs to be managed during the day time, and that nothing new is being created while they sleep. Context matters a lot.

100% passive income
I see this a lot with real estate educators, and it makes me laugh. Have you ever owned real estate? Have you ever had tenants? Have you ever dealt with brokers or contractors? As someone who has, let me be the first to tell you, it is completely **not** passive.

As a matter of fact, there is no such thing as a passive business. No such thing as passive real estate investing. The only thing passive is when you give your money to mutual funds or fund managers.

Saying something will be 100% passive or even "mostly" passive is definitely going to be a red-flag and will not win you any good will.

It takes just one click
This is also a flat out lie. Even my bank ATM machine requires at least ten clicks.

There is no context here. If you're saying this, you need to immediately delete it, and you need to check the rest of your marketing copy. Something tells me there will be many problems. The regulators will jump on this one and make a big issue of it because it's obviously just not true.

Nothing takes just one click, except maybe the decision to buy your course.

Use none of your own money (OPM)
When it comes to starting a business or securing a small business loan, you never really hear the term "other people's money" (OPM). But in real estate, and even fields like options trading, you hear it all the time.

Teaching someone to use other people's money is also the same as teaching them to go into debt. This can make the risk that someone takes on monumentally more than just buying your course. You could be wrecking lives. Taking on debt is something that should be done very carefully, and only by those who are very clear about what they're doing.

The FTC is not a fan of courses or claims around OPM. If you're going to teach people to use other people's money, I encourage you to make sure your copy is being very selective. You need to offer a lot of context, so you only attract accredited customers and go out of your way to protect those who just should not be going into debt.

Marketer's Perspective

Anik Singal

Here's the thing, most of us marketers don't mean harm. We don't mean to mislead or break rules. We just get excited. When we start selling, we get into it. We love what we're selling, and we want to get it into as many hands as possible. The sales side of us begins to overpromise a bit and perhaps "exaggerate just a little."

Well...

It's not just a little. Before we know it, it becomes a flat out lie. That's exactly why these terms create an impact and create challenges. Any one of us can step back, look at these terms, and instantly know we shouldn't be saying them.

Now, the frustration usually sets in from marketers.

"Anik, we basically can't say anything. What can we say?"

First, my next book is called "What You CAN Say," specifically to help with this.

Second, be honest. Don't talk about results you can't control. Talk about the product, the training, the experience, all things you can control.

I have news for you. It does convert. You just haven't tried it. You've built bad habits of wanting the "sexy" or the "hype." What you're not realizing is that consumers have changed. They've wisened up a lot in the last two decades.

The hype is actually deterring your best customers and attracting your worst customers. All these terms above should be removed. I did it, and my conversions stayed the same. However, the quality of my customers and the longevity of my business went sky high.

I've said it before, and I'll say it again. Compliant marketing is just a new muscle to practice. It works, You just have to fine-tune it and recalibrate. I promise.

Chapter 22:
Written-Sales Page Violations

Greg Christiansen

Before we get into the weeds a bit with some specific rules based on specific types of selling, I just want to emphasize that all the rules discussed above are universal. It doesn't matter if they're written on a sales page or spoken on a telephone.

However, each medium of selling does have some specific things to look for, in addition to the rules above. I want to use our closing chapters to go over those.

We'll start with written sales pages.

The Terms of Services Pages

Terms and conditions, which are commonly found at the bottom of websites and during sign-up processes, are vital. They not only inform your customers, but they protect the company. From a regulatory perspective, terms and conditions allow companies to clearly lay out the rules, requirements, and policies that users must agree to in order to access or use a product or service. They include:

1. Eligibility requirements to access or use a service
2. Acceptable and prohibited uses of the website/service
3. User content/submission policies and licenses
4. Privacy, data collection, and sharing policies

5. Service fees, billing policies, and auto-renewal terms
6. User account policies, including registration, termination, and suspensions
7. Rules and restrictions around contests, sweepstakes, or promotions
8. Procedures for copyright/trademark complaints and submissions
9. Disclaimers of warranties and limitations of liability for damages
10. Choice of law, jurisdiction, and dispute resolution procedures

These are just some examples of what a good terms and services page will cover. Think of this page as a contract between you and every visitor and customer. Many marketers ignore this page. They copy and paste the pages from other sites and think no one cares or reads it. Yet I haven't only seen this come up in many regulatory cases, but also many class-action and private lawsuits where the terms and conditions become a deciding factor.

Here's a unique benefit of a well-written terms and conditions page—protection against class-action lawsuits. You can actually insert simple clauses into your terms that seriously protect you, something I do with all my clients.

It will take little time to put this in but possibly provide millions in protection.

Don't copy and paste your terms and conditions. Invest in getting one created for your business that considers your location, your marketing practices, your products, how you deliver, your industry, and your risk exposure.

Get one tailored to your needs. Trust me.

Privacy Policy Pages

Much like terms and conditions establish the rules of engagement between businesses and users, privacy policies serve a specific regulatory purpose too—disclosing how consumer data is handled. This is one area that is getting a lot of attention lately, as people get more serious about their information. There are many FTC cases and other lawsuits that revolve around the use of consumer data, including what is disclosed and how.

From community sites to ecommerce stores to coaching programs, virtually all websites capture some form of personal information, such as:

- Name
- Email
- Phone
- Address
- IP Address
- Questions on a form

The question is how transparent are they with that data collection, usage, and sharing?

Enter the privacy policy.

An increasing number of laws now globally require websites to publish exactly what data they gather and how it may be disseminated. These include identifiers like:

- Geo-location
- Device details
- Contact information
- Browsing history

Don't Say That

Beyond listing these, an effective privacy policy specifies why such data is gathered; where it is stored; how to opt-out of collection; when it might be shared to third parties, like advertisers or business partners; and if/when it is ever deleted.

There is an endless list of cases that were led by the FTC, states, or even privately by consumers that are all about data usage and privacy. As with the terms page, I am baffled by how many people simply copy and paste a template privacy policy page. Later, they discover that the privacy policy didn't even cover their needs or their practices.

And now, they're in violation of not notifying their customers, which is a big offense.

In short, the right privacy policy protects users and covers companies legally. Generic templates found online seldom do. Get a custom one written that specifically caters to your marketing practices. You also want to make sure that you periodically revisit and edit it, as your marketing evolves and changes.

Contact Information

These days, a lot of websites try to get away with not having a contact page. Maybe they think an Instagram account or Twitter handle counts. Honestly, they also just don't want their customers contacting them, so they're hiding. And they're trying to reduce their expenses.

They hide the contact information and keep forcing people to use the FAQ or get lost on the site, looking for the contact information. Well, the FTC sees this as a violation and says that the site is potentially using "unfair or deceptive means" to limit complaints, refund requests, or general support.

In my experience, the more contact information you supply, the better. The easier you make it for someone to reach you, the better. However, as a minimum, I tell my clients to always have at least an email and physical address easily visible on the contact page.

Similar to privacy policies and terms pages, a real "Contact Us" page signifies you care about your customers and visitors. It means you stand behind your content, products, and claims enough to hear feedback. It builds trust and credibility.

I've seen the lack of contact pages trigger regulatory inquiries just as much as a lack of other compliance elements. The BBB even advises that contactability increases perceptions by enabling transparency.

Marketer's Perspective

Anik Singal

Remember, everything else applies. We just wanted to cover a few things that you need to have on your sales pages that may not show up on a webinar or telesales call (although the order pages must have what we say above).

You know how many times I search on Google and see people who have copied and pasted my terms and privacy policies? It's crazy. Now, congratulations to you if you have. There are some great terms in there. However, know this—you're in strict violation, and to top it off, you're at risk of me suing you.

It's not expensive nowadays. Hire a credible attorney. Take an hour to explain your business and what and how you collect information. Let them write something that will protect you and your specific business. It's worth every penny in the future.

Chapter 23:
Webinars & Video Sales Letters

Greg Christiansen

Webinars and video selling have taken off in the last decade. It went from being rare to being the primary way marketers sell their products. It started with video sales letters (VSLs), but now we're seeing a big trend for webinars.

It makes sense. They're a very effective tool. However, with increased competition and so many selling using video and webinars, I'm seeing marketers play a dangerous game of "who can be the least compliant?" Also, with webinars, if a marketer's on LIVE in a room for three to four hours, by default, the risk of saying something non-compliant skyrockets. To top it off, hype is increasing and marketers are saying more and more things to get better conversions than the next person.

This is also making webinars a key focus area for regulators. In the case of Lurn, the initial investigative document had quote after quote from multiple webinars that Lurn had hosted in the past (some that were three years old). It's abundantly clear that the regulators aren't just watching webinars; they're dissecting them, sentence-by-sentence.

Including the rules we've already discussed, here's a quick checklist of specific violations I see on webinars again and again:

- Falsifying claims of being LIVE
- Opening disclosure
- Testimonials
- Flamboyant self-stories
- Proximity disclosures
- Hypothetical calculations
- Fake charities
- Value stacking
- False scarcity

Some of these we've touched on already, but I want to explain why they matter in VSLs and webinars.

Falsifying claims of being LIVE (on Webinars)
This one is simple. Someone is watching an automated webinar that was recorded months ago. In the webinar, you're saying "I'm LIVE." But you're not. So, in the eyes of the regulators, you're lying, or as they say, misrepresenting.

You're calling out names, creating engagement, talking about how many seats are left, and each and every time you do that, you're lying. If you think about it from their perspective, it really does make sense. It's misrepresentation 101.

Sure, one can argue it's innocent, but nonetheless, it's considered deceptive, and they do give it importance.

> 33. These claims are false. The webinars are prerecorded and Defendants replay them for months at a time. These webinars make the same claims about nearing capacity, and about customers needing to act quickly to secure their spots regardless of when the webinar plays and how many consumers have enrolled at a particular time.

Image Source: FTC (2023)[17]

This is directly from the complaint letter against Lurn. Their automated webinars were flagged for claiming to be LIVE, while not being LIVE. It was important enough to make it into the complaint.

Opening disclosure

The way most webinars open is with a big claim. They read the headline and immediately go into testimonial stacks and lifestyle photos. They're doing this to create excitement and intrigue, but they're also creating the worst net impression from the beginning and just raising their non-compliance score.

Whereas, the right way to start is with a genuine disclosure. Right at the beginning. Unavoidable. Make sure that anyone and everyone that watches your presentation has to see the full disclosure.

It's not hard:

> "Everyone, before we begin I would like to do a little housekeeping. Today, I am going to go over several techniques and strategies. To explain these strategies, I like to use examples. Please note that these are examples only. They are not guarantees of success or that you should expect to see similar types of results. That would

---

[17] FTC. 2023. United States District Court for the District of Maryland. https://www.ftc.gov/system/files/ftc_gov/pdf/FiledLurnComplaint.pdf.

be impossible for me to promise, because everyone's journey with this is different.

I have no idea if you'll follow my techniques and strategies, or if you'll only watch this presentation and then take action on your own, disregarding my direction. In fact, there is no guarantee that my direction will work every time. There are always external factors that can affect my business activities.

But what we plan to do today is to show you how to identify certain risks, and how to hopefully avoid them. We also want to show you with our guidance, assistance, support, and training, how certain strategies can put you in the best position to succeed, while mitigating your risks. Again, as we go through this presentation, please note that your effort and application of concepts is essential."

Now, this doesn't mean you can do anything you want in the video or webinar. You still have to follow the rules, but by doing this disclosure clearly and honestly in the beginning, you're doing a great job laying a strong net impression foundation.

Testimonials

We covered this mostly in the testimonials section above, but I just want to highlight that I see testimonials being done non-compliantly a lot on webinars and videos, and the FTC is playing close attention.

Just to refresh your memory, using testimonials in your presentations requires the following four rules, with absolutely no exceptions:

1. Signed release and affidavit
2. Full substantiation for any claims made
3. Typicality of results
4. Disclosure proximity to the testimonial

You need to make sure you're not using outlier or crazy stories. The typicality of the results you're discussing on the testimonial is one of the hardest areas for marketers, yet it remains a primary target for regulators.

Remember, the FTC warning letters right now are centered around testimonial and endorsement usage. It's a clear indication of their priorities right now.

Flamboyant self-stories

So, you have great results. You want to share them with the market. And you can. Given a few very important factors, including:

- **They must be fully substantiated. Not kind of. Not close. Fully.**
  This means you need to be able to prove without a shadow of doubt that you actually have the results you're making claims on. The proof also needs to be recent and inarguable.
- **They need to be followed with context.**
  You have to disclose and disclaim tremendously clearly that the only reason you're sharing your own results is for credibility and not by any means implying that your results will be theirs. You've got a lot of experience and advantages.
- **Don't Overdo It**
  Give someone an inch, and they take an arm. I begrudgingly allow my clients to use their own results, because the minute I agree, they overdo it. So, if you want to share your own huge results, do it once or twice. Don't lean on it. Don't keep coming back to it. If you do, you're risking creating the wrong net impression, and then suddenly, even substantiated results are non-compliant.

Proximity disclosures

Many marketers put a disclosure at the beginning or in the middle, just once, and feel they're covered. The FTC is very clear on this. You need to make sure you have a visible, easily accessible or auditory disclosure within proximity to any claim you make—big or small.

If you have a testimonial, you need a disclosure.

If you tell your own story, you need a disclosure.

Wherever it shows up, you need a disclosure.

Hypothetical calculations
This is something I see on webinars a lot. Many times, it can be easy to pull out a spreadsheet and do a hypothetical example of how the business style creates income. There are projections made, numbers filled in, and in the end, the math shows how the prospect could potentially earn $12,568 a month if just X, Y, and Z happen.

On the outside, it seems okay. It's clearly hypothetical. It's even got a disclosure that it's for example purposes only.

Here's where the problem comes in. There's a "projected" $12,568 income at the end of the calculations. Unless there is a copious amount of context and disclosure, there is a very good chance that the net impression being created here can be seen as an implied earnings claim.

As a matter of fact, in the Lurn case, one of the product presentations had exactly this in it; a purely hypothetical example that led to a projection. The number they reached in the projection was $11,453 a month. Well, that number shows up again and again in their complaint letter. It's even quoted to be a projection, but in their eyes, it remains a violation.

Context matters.

Disclosures matter.

One of the most effective ways to use hypotheticals is to show a small example and not to focus on large figures, even if they're typical. Illustrating a chart where a client makes one Shopify sale or makes 3% in an investment is more effective, in many cases, than showing clients who do millions on Shopify or make 100% per month with an investment.

First, the smaller example seems more credible. Second, the consumer can relate more to the smaller example than a larger one. Plus, the small hypothetical comes under less scrutiny by regulatory bodies.

Proof of charitable donations
If you do charitable work, that's amazing. Please continue. If you decide to use that charitable work as a marketing tool in your promotions, please be careful. If you declare publicly that you've donated to causes or done philanthropic work, make sure to document it and have substantiation.

First of all, don't lie. I've seen too many clients who claim to make donations. They even raise the money from their audience and actually never donate. This is wrong on so many levels, but I won't address it any further here.

Secondly, assuming you do make donations, don't embellish or exaggerate them to make yourself look better. Using public work as a marketing tool is heavily audited in these investigations. It gets special attention. Third, keep proof of what you say. Specific and accurate proof.

Value stacking
We dedicated an entire chapter to this. I see fake value stacking the most on webinars. I would say that I have never reviewed a webinar that didn't have an end product that was said to be worth $10,000 or more.

Don't Say That

Again, if it's truly worth that much, and you have every ounce of documentation, say it. It's true. However, I've also never seen one where the documentation was there. Mostly, these numbers get made up by "subjective feelings."

Anik and many other clients have now tested hosting webinars with no value stacks, and the reports are that it makes no difference. Keep it honest. Keep it real. You still get customers, and even better, you get the right customers.

False scarcity
We dedicated an entire chapter to this too. Again, I would say that a large majority of the webinars I review have some form of false scarcity in them. These are some of the most common types:

- Offer closing in 30 minutes.
- Bonus for the first 100 only.
- I'm only going to let 200 students in.
- If you come back tomorrow, you won't get in.
- This price is only valid for 1 hour.

I've seen it all, and it's almost never true. Trust me, you can sell just fine without it. Take these out, unless you can factually prove they're true.

Marketer's Perspective
Anik Singal

GULP

I'll be the first to say that without any intention of harm, some of these things did make it into my past webinars. I honestly was just modeling what I'm used to seeing. I felt, if I was going to compete, I had to "hack" and "model." The habits were set more than a decade ago and just kept going.

I stand by the fact that I'm very proud of our products and our customer support. We delivered amazing courses. Regardless, the FTC is not worried about that. The rules are the rules. They watched my webinars and pulled out words and sentences that violated their rules.

Listen, I get it.

When we do what we do, we are just trying to help someone make a decision. We believe in what we're selling, and we don't believe we're hurting anyone. But in the end, it's not right; it's not allowed. I've since done many webinars without any of these things, and the results are amazing. Yes, compliant webinars do work, and you get far better customers and even better sleep at night.

You just have to take time to practice and learn a new way.

Chapter 24:
Tele-Sales Violations

Greg Christiansen

We dedicated a lot of this book to discussing the changes that happened in 2021 in the way the FTC regulates. The AMG case ruling in the Supreme Court has made it so the FTC is now focusing more on Section 19 and the application of the Telemarketing Sales Rule.

This basically means that, if you have a "one-on-one" (also known as telesales) operation, you're at greater regulatory risk. This doesn't mean you shouldn't have a phone sales team; it just means that you need to administer the rules and monitor the team very closely.

In addition to the rules already discussed, let's go over some of the things I constantly hear on sales calls that are problematic:

- Proper introduction
- Fake titles or credibility for the sales person
- Cooling-off period (Rights of Recission)
- Pushy & unprofessional selling
- Creating success
- Goal-setting
- Clear disclosures
- Overselling the refund or guarantee
- Legal & tax advice
- Hidden phone numbers & ringless voicemails

Proper introduction

At the very beginning of every sales call, there must be a formal introduction with the name of the caller, who or what company they represent, the purpose of the call, and whether the call is being recorded.

The salesperson has to use their real name, no fake names or aliases allowed. They have to be forthcoming on why they're calling, who they're representing, and how they got their information, if asked.

For example, if I was one of Anik's salespeople, I would say, "My name is Greg Christiansen, calling on behalf of Lurn. I noticed your recent book purchase online, and I'm calling on a recorded line to make sure you're happy and to offer any further assistance. How are you today?"

Pretty easy. However, this introduction is missed on many calls that I review.

Fake titles or credibility for the sales person

If you're speaking with the CEO of a company, versus someone from their sales team, it goes without saying the CEO will have a higher conversion rate. The CEO has authority, and the person on the other line feels special to be speaking to someone in their position. This has led to some sales teams giving their sales associates fake titles that puff up their role in the company. For example, Director of Sales.

I was sitting in a deposition one time, when the FTC attorney asked the CEO a question:

"In this telephone call, your agent claims that he is the Director of Sales. Is he?" The CEO fumbled around a bit and tried to defend it by saying yes. The attorney from the FTC already had an org chart in his hand and threw it on the table and asked, "Can you point to the org chart and show me?"

The truth was that the sales agent was just that, an associate. But he'd lied on the phone and given himself some inflated title to help him close more deals.

In short, don't do that.

Give your real title and don't misrepresent it.

Cooling-off period (Rights of Rescission)
We had an entire chapter dedicated to this too, but it's very relevant to programs sold one-on-one, especially the ones that are thousands of dollars. Your agent must absolutely inform the customer of the cooling-off period, or the sale can be seen as refundable at any time in the future, meaning the refund window is infinitely open.

Federal law demands three days to let the customer change their mind. State law varies, but the allowable window to change their mind can be five or seven days in some states.

The customer must be clearly aware, whether they are told on the phone, in a written contract, or even on their receipt. It's the responsibility of the business to inform the customer.

Pushy & unprofessional selling
There's no official rule written in the regulatory books about unprofessional selling. However, I've been in countless meetings with regulators and have seen how the air in the room changed after they heard some nasty calls.

If they hear the sales agent bullying the customer, yelling at them, pressuring them, being condescending or forcing a sale, the entire investigation is going to get worse. The outcome will have less leniency, and the regulators will be far less likely to move on anything.

If a customer is not buying, let it be. End the call and live to fight another day. Because chastising the customer or bullying them is going to get you and your business into major hot water.

Creating success

"You're lucky. We're really going to pour into you because I want you to become one of our key success stories that we can promote in the future. So, you're going to get more from us!"

Who doesn't want to create a success story, and who doesn't want to be a success story? I hear sales agents create this fake exclusivity and aura of special attention a lot. It gets noted by the regulators as well, and they'll be quick to ask what made that customer or sale more special.

If you're simply putting that customer into your normal delivery process, you've misrepresented and created a net impression that is false.

Goal-setting

This one got its chapter because it was something that became pivotal in Anik's case, and there is absolutely no public documentation of it. I only know about this from being inside many rooms with the FTC and hearing the leadership tell me this themselves:

"If you're goal-setting, that is an implied earnings claim, and it is a violation."

Do not set monetary goals that you can't substantiate with typical result studies. Talk about your product, their experience, and leave the results to a higher force. Even if the customer brings up their goals on their own, it is your responsibility to remind them of your purpose, and that you're in no way implying or guaranteeing them any results.

Clear disclosures

If a customer says, "I can't wait to make $10,000 a month with this," can you just let them say it and move on?

No.

It's your job on the phone to always make sure to disclose and correct. If something is said, even by the customer, that is not compliant or the customer makes it clear that they have the wrong net impression, you need to step in and correct it.

Disclosures don't just happen at the beginning of the call. You need to keep bringing them up whenever appropriate.

Overselling the refund or guarantee

I've seen people oversell the refund or even the right of rescission to rush the customers into making a purchase. They'll say, "What do you have to lose? It's totally risk free. You can always get your money back. You have time to think about it, but let's make a decision today."

Regardless of how easy the refund is, and that they've disclosed the right to recission, the regulators heavily frown on any company that leans on these things to close a sale. This starts to feel like a misrepresented and uninformed sale. It also attracts the wrong type of customers, who turn right around and have buyer's remorse.

It's required that you tell them about the refund period, but leave it at that. Don't make it a major selling point.

Legal & tax advice

This is one that always shocks me. Giving legal or tax advice when you're not qualified can get you into a lot of trouble with advertising regulators, but also organizations that oversee lawyers and accountants. This is also the fastest way to get a class-action or consumer lawsuit.

Here's an example of sales agents giving advice that became financial advice, and now, the SEC is stepping in. In a specific case, the sales agents were charging $40,000 to create automated Amazon stores. What they would do on the phone is convince customers to use their 401k funds to start the store. This officially classifies as investment advice, and now the SEC is taking the lead on the case.

"Let's get this business started. You can deduct the cost of this entire program on your taxes. You can deduct your home because it's a home office. You have so many tax benefits, even if you don't make a dollar."

That advice can only come from a CPA or a tax lawyer. Yet it can be heard on many sales calls.

"Let's set-up your estate immediately. Once your funds are there, your wife can never touch them if you get divorced."

Again, if you're not a certified financial planner, estate attorney, or certified CPA, giving this advice is illegal.

Make sure to monitor your sales agents closely to assure they're not stepping out of their lane to give advice that only the qualified professionals should be. This is a major area of potential legal issues in the future.

Hidden phone numbers & ringless voicemails

We're entering into dual agency territory now. The FCC and FTC and even states. There is a lot of activity around the rules to be able to call and text prospects. Your phone number, robo-dialing, A.I. voices all have strict rules coming out that are in favor of the consumer.

If you send even one text message outside the law, the receiving consumer can easily sue you. I have seen case after case of this. There are attorneys who specialize in helping administer these calls, and the laws are only getting more stringent with:

- Ringless voicemails
- Telephone calls
- Robocalls
- A.I. calls
- Text messages
- Voice notes

Written permission is needed. Timing of calls and how often you can call them in a certain period is now dictated. These rules are evolving daily and states are starting to step up and have their own regulations. If you have webinars that send out text messages or sales agents that make phone calls, you need to get compliant fast because there is going to be a barrage of regulators and private law suits coming in this area.

Marketer's Perspective
Anik Singal

Well, what can I say? I thought I was doing it right? I had a full-time paralegal. We listened to every sales call that led to a sale. We scored them. We held weekly meetings. We did weekly summaries and training.

I followed the rules as best as we knew them. We didn't break any of them, except the one that we had no idea about—goal setting.

I can tell you from personal experience, if I didn't have the telesales operation, and if we didn't ask people what their goals were, my case would have been incredibly different. It's unfortunate for me, but a win for you. Telesales are a great way to drive revenue, and I will still have it as a part of my business, but I will also monitor it much closer and assure that my agents are completely compliant. No room for error there.

Chapter 25:
Recurring Sales Violations

Greg Christiansen

Recurring income is becoming vital for businesses to succeed. Everyone wants secure month-over-month revenue. However, the challenge is that consumers are petrified of making recurring commitments. It makes selling these programs hard.

Unfortunately, this ends up making marketers more aggressive.

A lot of marketers solve the problem by getting tricky. They begin using trial offers. They begin hiding terms for recurring. They begin adding recurring as upsells, where consumers don't even realize what they're committing to.

In the end, many companies become reliant on the hope that the consumer will just forget they even subscribed, and the offer will keep rebilling month-over-month right under their nose. Well, the FTC and other regulators have received enough complaints about this that they've made it one of their primary focal points to enforce transparency and honesty.

Recurring sales are administered and regulated under something called the "Restore Online Shoppers Confidence Act" (ROSCA). It began to get aggressive in 2009, when the FTC started investigating a company called Google Treasure Chest (also known by a lot of other names). This was a subscription service that promised customers easy ways to make money online. Their ads featured giant checks and luxurious lifestyles and were swimming with testimonials. Part of the problem was that they were making a lot of fake earnings claims, but the bigger problem was the fraudulent strategies they were using to get people into multiple subscription services.

Customers thought they were doing a one-time purchase of something very low-cost. However, this company would hide the continuity in the terms. Not only that, but they would then sign them up for many subscriptions, all of varying prices. The customer had no idea how many, which ones, or even how to get out of them. This drew the attention not only of the FTC, but also VISA, Mastercard, and AMEX, all wanting to heavily regulate continuity programs.

As a result, in 2010, Congress passed ROSCA to better regulate the rules around subscriptions. ROSCA covers continuity plans, automatic renewals, free-to-pay conversion sales, and negative options.

Since then, there have been many more examples of companies being cited for ROSCA violations. For example, Vonage had to pay $100 million dollars to settle the FTC complaint that it wouldn't let customers cancel their service.

FTC Action Against Vonage Results in $100 Million to Customers Trapped by Illegal Dark Patterns and Junk Fees When Trying to Cancel Service

Vonage will be required to provide a simple way to cancel

Image Source: FTC (2022)[18]

---

[18] FTC. 2022. FTC Action Against Vonage Results in $100 million to Customers Trapped by Illegal Dark Patterns and Junk Fees When Trying to Cancel Service. https://www.ftc.gov/news-events/news/press-releases/2022/11/ftc-action-against-vonage-results-100-million-customers-trapped-illegal-dark-patterns-junk-fees-when-trying-cancel-service.

Vonage made it very difficult for customers to cancel, and this led to a swarm of complaints that eventually cost them $100 million under ROSCA.

There are many companies that are being found to be out of compliance. Big companies and small businesses alike. Adoreme is an online clothing company that ran into problems with its membership service too. They used a negative option (assuming that consumers who were not specifically opting out of their subscriptions were, by default, agreeing to them) after customers enrolled in a VIP program to get access to new fashion trends. The FTC describes the plan in its complaint:

> 10. Membership in Defendant's VIP program offers consumers a discount on an initial purchase, discounted prices on apparel purchases, a free apparel set after five full-price purchases, free and unlimited product exchanges, free shipping for U.S. customers, and access to a "free personalized online showroom" of apparel for sale, including "VIP only" apparel, with "[n]o obligation to buy every month, [and] no membership fee."
>
> 11. Consumers join the VIP program on a negative option basis. Every month, Defendant charges each program member $39.95 – unless, in the first five days of each month, that member "shops" and buys apparel from Defendant or affirmatively clicks a button on Defendant's website or mobile Internet app to "skip" buying that month. If a VIP does not "shop or skip" during that five-day period, Defendant charges her or him for a $39.95 "store credit"

Image source: FTC (2017)[19]

As you can see here, the problem is that the rules of recurring fees are very complicated, and the way in which customers were tricked into subscribing is frowned upon.

---

[19] FTC. 2017. United States District Court Southern District of New York. https://www.ftc.gov/system/files/documents/cases/adoreme_complaint.pdf

Here's what ROSCA is and the guidelines to follow. In a nutshell, ROSCA sets specific rules around post-transaction practices for any business that wants to have a service or product that has a recurring charge. The biggest things prohibited are:

- Charging extra without clear consent
- Hiding negative option specifics
- Misrepresenting "free" trials and opt-outs
- Obscuring terms around gift cards

Opposed to what most marketers do, here are some specific rules that ROSCA says are absolutely not allowed:

- Pre-ticked boxes signing up customers for extra services
- Hard-to-locate confirmations and disclaimers
- No more questionable tricks at the last second

It all comes down to "if it's a tricky way to get someone to pay you, there's a good chance it's illegal under ROSCA."

Marketer's Perspective

Anik Singal

This makes sense to me. I have no issue with ROSCA and never have. As a matter of fact, back in 2010, when this apparent Google Treasure Chest case happened, I was doing millions a year with recurring programs.

Even before Google Treasure Chest, I had products that I would sell trials to and then they would go into $97 a month recurring. At one point, I had over 10,000 people paying me monthly. However, I never played any tricks. Our customers always knew exactly what they were paying and the terms. We also made cancellation very easy.

I remember the day the FTC took a hard hammer at trial-based companies. I even remember our merchant account kicking many merchants out. I was scared I would be next, and I immediately stopped selling all my programs. I even got a phone call from a Vice President at the bank who confirmed I was doing it correctly, saying, "You're not on any watch list Anik. You can keep selling."

But I was so scared of getting in trouble with the FTC, I immediately stopped, and I moved on. That was when I discovered webinars, selling high-ticket, and selling on the phone. The irony today is that I left a business model I was doing great in because of the fear of the FTC and walked right into a model that eventually got me in trouble with the FTC.

Remember, there is nothing wrong or illegal about recurring subscription-based revenue. Just make sure you practice full disclosure. Don't be tricky and let customers cancel easily. It's not hard at all.

Conclusion

First, congratulations on finishing this book and taking compliance seriously. We both know this is not easy. Learning to market compliantly means you have to unlearn quite a few habits from possibly decades of practice. However, unlike many marketers and advertisers, you've shown the desire and dedication and started the journey with us by first reading this book.

The truth is that compliant marketing is not an option or a choice. Regulators are getting more and more active by the day. And now, you'll notice that even consumers are getting more active with class-action and private lawsuits.

The only way to sleep well at night and to grow and scale your business safely is to know that you are doing so compliantly.

The other good news is that we have both now helped many businesses change their ways. As long as they're 100% committed and give it time, we're noticing that these businesses are seeing almost no difference in their conversions. They're growing and converting, all while bringing in far better customers and facing far less legal trouble.

But yes, it will take time. You'll need to practice and be very intentional about marketing within the guidelines we covered in this book. And it goes without saying that working with us, and allowing us to help you, will make your journey much easier.

We want to end with a brief summary of some of the key things we recommend you start with. Going fully compliant is a big exercise, so here are the key areas to focus on first:

1. **Substantiate your claims**

    Go through all your marketing. Any place you make any definitive or absolute statements about your results, or the results of your customers, seek substantiation right away. Do you have the proof? If not, immediately remove it.

2. **Testimonial usage**

    Testimonials are currently a big focus for the FTC. You need to follow the testimonial guidelines that we've given in this book. Remember, there are four rules, and all your testimonials must follow all four rules, or those testimonials need to be removed immediately.

3. **Using telesales or recurring sales**

    The FTC and other regulators are most focused on these two areas right now. Start by buttoning up these operations immediately and making them fully compliant. You need to make sure you have very firm practices to monitor your sales calls. Have a look at what our software Complily.com can do for you. You need to make sure you're closely monitoring the various complaint websites, such as BBB, Trust Pilot, Google Reviews, and others because having complaints is by far the easiest way to come under the eyes of the regulators. Remember, the complaints don't need to go directly to the FTC for them to get brought in. Keep everything out of the Sentinel system.

The easiest way to reduce your complaints is to make sure you have a liberal refund policy. Don't make them jump through hoops. Don't put "no refund policies" together. If someone is unhappy and is insisting on a refund, give it. And if your refund rate is getting too high, fix your product instead of making it harder on the customer. This is by far one of the easiest ways to reduce your complaints. But remember, this alone will not protect you. Your marketing still needs to be compliant.

So, start here. Do these things immediately, and your net impression score will take a big jump in the right direction. Remember, we also don't want you to walk around scared and shaking. We're not here to say that if you break any of the rules we have mentioned in the book, you'll immediately get sued by the FTC. If that were true, 10,000+ companies would get sued daily. It all comes down to your net impression.

Think of it this way—you have an empty glass in front of you. That means you're not in business. So, you're not violating any laws because you're not marketing. Now, what happens is, over time, as you start marketing, more and more people will begin to engage with your marketing.

Now, every single time you violate one of the rules in this book, it's like you're adding a drop of water into this empty glass. If you market very aggressively and on a big scale, the glass will fill up much faster. And imagine that when the glass overflows, the regulators come knocking. The best way is to just follow the rules and know that no water is getting added into your glass.

Our goal is simple. We want to spread the good news of compliance. We want you to grow. We want you to scale. And we want you to sleep well at night while doing it.

As for Anik, he only has one message for you:

> "I don't want anyone to ever experience the hell I did. Nothing you're doing today, no money that you're making today, is worth it. Make your marketing compliant. Do it now. Please."

We're not done by the way. We have many more resources for you:

1. **DontSayThat.com**: We have our weekly podcast here for you to keep learning and stay in touch with all the legal updates in the marketing world.
2. **NAOAC.com**: Join our "National Association of Advertising Compliance" and be on the inside. We also have academies, employee training programs, certification programs, LIVE events, and so much more.
3. **Complily.com**: Fully A.I. powered software to monitor all your compliance, day and night. We can watch over all your ads, your sales messaging, your sales calls, your social media, your complaints. Let us help watch your back.

Thank you for letting us serve you through this book. Please feel free to engage with us and send us your questions. We're always here to help. We can be reached at: authors@dontsaythat.com.

Peace, Love & Compliance.

Greg & Anik

Appendix: Important Cases

This appendix includes some notable cases from the Federal Trade Commission (FTC) that every marketer should be aware of. These cases illustrate many of the key points we've discussed in this book.

In this appendix, you'll find summaries of these important FTC cases. We've done our best to pick out the most crucial information to help you understand each case better.

You can find the latest version of the appendix here: www.DONTSAYTHAT.com/appendix

Remember, these summaries are just a starting point. If you really want to get into the details and understand everything about a case, we suggest checking out the complaint and other documents filed in the case. This will give you a better picture of what actually happened.

Advocare International

Company: Advocare International, L.P
Date: October, 2019
Complaint: www.DONTSAYTHAT.com/advocare

Settlement:
$150 million judgment. Permanent ban on multi-level marketing. All distributors were notified about the FTC lawsuit and settlement.

Summary:
AdvoCare is a multi-level marketing company that promotes health and wellness products. Their participants earn money by selling AdvoCare products and recruiting additional participants.

The defendants were accused of operating an illegal pyramid scheme. The reason for this was the program's heavy emphasis on recruiting new participants.

The FTC accused the defendants of misleading earnings claims. Participants were under the impression that they were likely to make a lot of money when, according to the FTC, the overwhelming majority didn't make any money at all.

The materials the company distributed to recruit new participants also allegedly contained false or misleading representations.

Agora

Company: Agora Financial, LLC
Date: February, 2021
Complaint: www.DONTSAYTHAT.com/agora

Settlement:
More than $2 million. Restrictions on what kinds of representations can be made in the future.

Summary:
Agora is a Baltimore-based publisher. One of the publications they promoted was *The Doctor's Guide to Reversing Diabetes in 28 Days.*

The FTC claims that Agora and its affiliates tricked seniors into buying pamphlets, newsletters, and other publications that falsely promised a cure for type 2 diabetes. The publication claimed a "100% success rate," which the FTC is an improper claim based on the available evidence.

The FTC also claims that Agora and its affiliates promoted a plan to help them cash in on a government-affiliated check program. This would lead to a recurring annual charge for an investment newsletter called *Lifetime Income Report*. The FTC claimed multiple misrepresentations of these products in their marketing.

AMG Capital Management

Company: AMG Services, Inc
Date: March, 2015
Complaint: www.DONTSAYTHAT.com/amgcapital

Outcome:
$535 million in refund checks were sent to customers. The Supreme Court significantly curtailed the FTC's authority to use Section 13(b) to seek monetary relief. The case is still ongoing.

Settlement:
$505 million in refund checks were sent to customers. The Supreme Court significantly curtailed the FTC's authority to use Section 13(b) to seek monetary relief.

Summary:
AMG Capital Management offered payday loans. These loans were offered through a series of websites owned by the defendants.

The FTC alleged that the defendants misled their customers about the terms of their leans. They said they would charge borrowers the loan amount plus a one-time finance fee. Instead, the defendants made multiple withdrawals from consumers' bank accounts and assessed a new finance fee with each withdrawal. This meant that consumers paid more for the loans than they expected to pay.

The FTC also alleged that the defendants intimidated customers by threatening arrest or legal action if their debts were not paid.

The FTC used Section 13(b) authority to seek customer restitution. The case ended up in the Supreme Court, which ruled that Section 13(b) does not authorize the FTC to seek monetary restitution in court.

The case is still ongoing. The FTC is attempting to apply Section 19 violations against the defendants.

Automators, LLC (aka Empire Ecommerce)

Company: Automaters, LLC (Formerly known as Empire Ecommerce)
Date: August, 2023
Complaint: www.DONTSAYTHAT.com/automators

Settlement:
Judgment of $21,765,902.65. Partially suspended after defendants turn over assets, including multiple bank and cryptocurrency accounts. Permanent ban on offering business opportunities or coaching for e-commerce platforms. Prohibition on certain business practices.

Summary:
The defendants sold a program where customers could invest in "automated online stores," which they created and ran. Initially, they sold this program under Empire LLC, but after the online stores they started and ran were shut down, they restarted the program under the name Automators AI.

The FTC claimed that the defendants made multiple misrepresentations. They were accused of misrepresenting their backgrounds, including claims of being an "8-figure Amazon entrepreneur." They were also accused of making false earnings claims and improperly using testimonials to create unrealistic earning expectations.

The FTC claimed that the defendants misrepresented their use of artificial intelligence, claiming that students were using it to achieve "over $10,000/month in sales!"

Finally, the FTC accused the defendants of claiming that they were backed by "venture capital," even though no venture capital firm invested money into the business.

According to the FTC, most customers lost money. 70-80% of customer service inquiries were complaints. They said the defendants consistently denied refund requests and even threatened legal action against customers.

Comcast & DIRECTV

Company: DIRECTV and Comcast, Corp
Date: April, 2009
Complaint: www.DONTSAYTHAT.com/comcast | www.DONTSAYTHAT.com/directv2

Settlement:
DIRECTV paid $2.31 million. Comcast paid $900,000. Defendants are prohibited from future violations of the Telemarketing Sales Rule and Do Not Call Rule.

Summary:
The FTC accused both companies of violating the Do Not Call provisions of the Telemarketing Sales Rule. This included charges that they called consumers who had specifically told the companies not to call them again.

In addition, they were accused of improperly making calls that did not connect to a live person.

DIRECTV had settled a separate case in 2005 when it was accused of violating the Do Not Call order.

DIRECTV
Company: DIRECTV
Date: March, 2015
Complaint: www.DONTSAYTHAT.com/directv

Settlement:
The FTC dropped its charges against DIRECTV after a federal judge rejected their attempt to get $4 billion in customer restitution.

Summary:
DIRECTV provides direct-to-home digital television services. These are offered by subscription. DIRECTV offered new customers low introductory pricing, which would increase after a certain amount of time. New customers are often locked into 24-month contracts with a cancellation fee.

The FTC alleged that DIRECTV failed to adequately disclose to consumers that its low introductory pricing lasted just one year but tied buyers to a two-year contract. This violated the Restore Online Shoppers' Confidence Act (ROSCA).

The FTC also alleged that the defendants failed to alert customers that its offer for 90 days of premium channels required them to cancel the subscription to avoid continuing monthly charges.

Originally, the FTC sought $4 billion for customer restitution, claiming that all customers had been deceived. A federal judge dismissed rejected this argument, and the FTC dismissed the remaining charges.

Digital Altitude

Company: Digital Altitude, LLC
Date: February, 2018
Complaint: www.DONTSAYTHAT.com/digitalaltitude

Settlement:
$54 million judgment against the defendants. This was suspended due to inability to pay. Defendants have various restrictions on their business practices.

Summary:
Digital Altitude created a program to help customers make money working from home. Digital Altitude offered multiple membership tiers. Customers are paid when new customers join the program through commissions based on new customers' membership fees.

The FTC accused Digital Altitude of using deceptive sales practices. They were accused of using earnings claims without substantiation. They ran ads saying customers would "make six figures online in the next ninety days or less." According to the FTC, this was not the typical experience of Digital Altitude customers.

The FTC claimed Digital Altitude misrepresented the "coaching" they offered at lower membership levels. They were designed primarily to convince customers to purchase higher-tier memberships, while the "coaches" were actually salespeople paid on commission.

Regulators claimed that Digital Altitude had high chargeback rates and had merchant accounts canceled.

DK Automation

Company: DK Automation
Date: November, 2022
Complaint: www.DONTSAYTHAT.com/dkautomation

Settlement:
Judgment of almost $53 million, suspended after payment of $2.6 million, along with additional ongoing payments. Prohibitions on certain practices around earnings claims, misrepresentations, and more.

Summary:
The defendants sold done-for-you programs around building a business on Amazon. They promised to help set up an Amazon store for customers, identify profitable products, negotiate with suppliers, and order, process, and ship inventory to Amazon. They also promised ongoing management of the stores.

The FTC's first accusation was that the defendants used false and unsubstantiated earnings claims. They created the impression that customers would earn a substantial profit when in reality, that was not the typical experience.

The FTC also accused the defendants of using unfair tactics to discourage customers from speaking out about the program. They were also accused of falsifying positive reviews and artificially removing negative reviews.

The defendants were also accused of violating the Business Opportunity Rule by not providing proper disclosures.

FBA Stores
Company: AWS, LLC
Date: March, 2018
Complaint: www.DONTSAYTHAT.com/fbastores

Settlement:
Judgment of $63.5 million, partially suspended after $2.55 million in funds and assets are surrendered. Defendants are banned from marketing and selling business opportunities and business coaching programs.

Summary:
The defendants created the Amazing Wealth System, a program to help customers create an online business by selling products on Amazon. The focus was on being a third-party seller.

The FTC accused the defendants of making false and unsubstantiated earnings claims. Their marketing and sales implied that customers using the system would make substantial money. According to the FTC, the defendants couldn't substantiate those claims.

While they had disclaimers that said that results were not guaranteed, the FTC did not deem them sufficient. According to the FTC, prospects' net impression was that they would profit from the system.

The FTC also accused the defendants of failing to provide prospects with the disclosure documents required by the Business Opportunity Rule.

Herbalife
Company: Herbalife International of America, Inc
Date: July, 2016
Complaint: www.DONTSAYTHAT.com/herbalife

Settlement:
Judgment of $200 million. Ban on selling money-making opportunities. Prohibits certain business practices around multi-level compensation,

preferred customer categories, collection of retail sales information, sales verification, refund policies, and more.

Summary:
Herbalife is a multi-level marketing business opportunity in which participants sell weight management, nutritional supplements, and personal care products and recruit new participants into the program. They are compensated for selling the product and enrolling new participants.

The defendants were accused of unfair practices, mainly by creating a compensation structure that emphasized recruiting new members rather than selling products.

The defendants were also accused of misleading income claims. The FTC also claimed that these income claims were not substantiated. According to them, most customers didn't make any money even though they were led to believe that they would.

Infusion Media, Inc (aka Google Money Tree)
Company: Infusion Media, Inc
Date: June, 2009
Complaint: www.DONTSAYTHAT.com/infusion

Settlement:
Judgment of $29.5 million; partially suspended with $3.5 million in cash and other assets. Ban on selling products through "negative option" transactions. In 2014, the defendant was found to have misrepresented his financials and became liable for the full judgment.

Summary:
The defendants sold home business opportunity "kits." These kits went by multiple names, including "Google Money Tree." They claimed to help customers make money from home by "just filling out forms and running searches on Google and Yahoo."

The kits are shipped for a small fee. Customers gave their credit card information to receive the kits. They were automatically enrolled into a membership program and would be charged a recurring fee unless they proactively canceled.

The FTC alleged that this automatic enrollment was not adequately disclosed and that money was charged without proper authorization.

In addition, the defendants were alleged to have made false income claims and improperly implied that they were associated with Google.

Intuit (TurboTax)

Company: Intuit, Inc
Date: March, 2022
Complaint: www.DONTSAYTHAT.com/turbotax

Option & Final Order:
Intuit is prohibited from advertising or marketing that any good or service is free unless it's free for all customers or it discloses clearly & conspicuously and in close proximity to the "free" claim the percentage of taxpayers or consumers who qualify for the free version. There are some additional requirements around disclosure.

Summary:
This was an administrative complaint.

TurboTax is a tax preparation software that allows customers to prepare and file their income tax returns. For many years, ads promoting TurboTax touted its free tax filing option, which is limited to specific tax returns (Mainly for people with only W-2 income). Some of their ads consisted almost entirely of the word "free" spoken repeatedly.

The FTC sued Intuit over its ads pitching free TurboTax products. Intuit claimed that customers would be misled by the ads and be under the impression that they could get their taxes prepared for free. According to the commission, this was deceptive since about two-thirds of tax filers in 2020 would have been ineligible for the company's free offerings.

For example, freelance workers who received 1099 forms could not use the free version of TurboTax.

There were disclaimers in the ads, but the FTC said that they were difficult to see and that reasonable consumers would still believe that TurboTax products would be free for them.

Ivy Capital

Company: Ivy Capital, Inc
Date: February, 2011
Complaint: www.DONTSAYTHAT.com/ivycapital

Settlement:
$130 million judgment against the corporate and individual defendants. This is suspended upon surrendering their assets, including two homes and eight cars. Defendants are banned from marketing and selling business coaching programs.

Summary:
Ivy Capital sold programs that claimed to help customers create their own online businesses from home. Consumers paid between $2,000 and $20,000 for a business coaching program, the price of which, the FTC claims, was based on the amount of funds customers had available.

Telemarketing practices were a major part of the case. The FTC accused the defendants of contacting leads on the National Do Not Call Registry. During the calls, they were accused of using high-pressure sales tactics.

Some specific practices they were accused of were false scarcity, false qualification, improper use of testimonials, and making implied earnings claims.

Ivy Capital's refund policies were also criticized. They had a strict 3-day refund policy, but this policy was not always disclosed. In addition, some customers complained that they were unable to receive a refund even if they requested it in the 3-day window.

John Beck Amazing Profits
Company: John Beck Amazing Profits, LLC
Date: June, 2009
Complaint: www.DONTSAYTHAT.com/johnbeck

Settlement:
$478 million judgment. Ban on infomercials and telemarketing. Restrictions on what kinds of claims can be made in the future.

Summary:
John Beck Amazing Profits, LLC sold written materials, CD's, DVD's and coaching programs about real estate investing. They primarily sold their products through infomercials and telesales.

The FTC claimed that the defendants misrepresented the likelihood of success with their system. They also claimed that there were earnings claims and that customers would quickly earn back what they had invested.

In addition, the FTC claimed that the defendants did not properly disclose that customers were automatically enrolled in a continuity membership program. Customers had to take affirmative action to cancel their memberships, or they would be charged.

The FTC also accused the defendants of initiating outbound telephone calls to customers who previously said that they didn't want to receive them.

KFC Corporation
Company: KFC Corporation
Date: June, 2004
Complaint: www.DONTSAYTHAT.com/kfc

Settlement:
KFC is prohibited from making claims about its chicken products' nutritional value, weight loss benefits, or other health benefits that it cannot substantiate.

Summary:
This was an administrative case. The KFC Corporation owned the Kentucky Fried Chicken national restaurant chain.

The FTC accused KFC of making false claims in a national advertising campaign. The company was accused of making unsubstantiated claims about its fried chicken's nutritional value, weight-loss benefits, and other health benefits.

One of the advertisements that the FTC flagged claimed that eating KFC fried chicken was healthier than eating a Burger King Whopper. Another said that eating fried chicken was compatible with a low-carb diet.

Mike Rando
Company: Prosperity Training Technology LLC, among others
Date: May, 2022
Complaint: www.DONTSAYTHAT.com/rando

Settlement:
Judgment of $18,875,613. Partially suspended after turning over numerous real estate investments, cars, and the contents of numerous bank,

investment, and life insurance accounts. Permanent ban on offering credit repair services and making unsubstantiated claims.

Summary:
The defendants offered credit repair services called "The Credit Game." The program claimed to legally improve customer's credit scores. A prominent strategy was "credit piggybacking," which involves becoming an authorized user on someone else's credit cards. There was also a business opportunity program involving creating your own credit repair service.

The FTC made multiple accusations of misrepresentation against the defendants. They were accused of misrepresenting the likelihood of improving credit scores, misrepresenting the legality of the methods taught, such as "credit piggybacking," and of misrepresenting the earning potential of creating your own credit repair service.

In addition, the FTC accused the defendants of misrepresenting their money-back guarantee. They claimed that customers had the impression that they could request refunds for all products or services offered by the defendants but were told they couldn't get refunded for credit repair services.

The FTC also accused the defendants of violating the Credit Repair Organizations Act by not giving proper disclosures and improperly collecting customer fees.

MOBE

Company: MOBE, Ltd
Date: June, 2018
Complaint: www.DONTSAYTHAT.com/mobe

Settlement:
Judgment of over $318 million. Over $17 million was paid as a part of the settlement. Ban on sale of business coaching and investment opportunities.

Summary:
My Online Business Education (MOBE) was a Malaysian company that offered a program that showed customers how to start their own online business quickly. This program was based on a 21-step system. There were multiple levels of membership, starting at $49 and rising to multiple thousands of dollars.

The FTC accused MOBE of using false and unsubstantiated earnings claims to sell their programs. MOBE had disclosures, but they were not prominently displayed.

The defendants were also accused of misleading customers about their refund policy. The FTC claimed customers were under the impression that memberships were refundable without conditions. However, conditions for refunds were imposed post-purchase. Refunds were often denied, and chargebacks were disputed.

Nissan Truck

Company: Nissan North America, Inc; TBWA Worldwide, Inc
Date: January, 2014
Complaint: www.DONTSAYTHAT.com/nissan

Settlement:
The defendants are prohibited from using deceptive demonstrations in advertisements for pickup trucks.

Summary:
This was an administrative case.

Nissan is a company that sells pickup trucks, among other vehicles. TBWA is an advertising company.

A television ad depicted a Nissan truck rescuing a dune buggy trapped in sand on a steep hill. The truck was shown pushing the dune buggy up the hill, which is not something that the vehicle can do. According to the complaint, the dune buggy was dragged up the hill by cables.

The FTC also alleged that special effects were used to make the hill look steeper than it was. In summary, the FTC alleged that the ad created a misleading impression of what the truck can do.

Nudge

Company: Nudge, LLC
Date: November, 2019
Complaint: www.DONTSAYTHAT.com/nudge

Settlement:
Judgment of $16.7 million. Ban on selling money-making opportunities.

Summary:
This case was brought by the FTC and the Utah Division of Consumer Protection.

The defendants sold real estate training programs. They said their system would show customers how to find property at discounted prices, avoid putting their own money down, and gain access to individual investors who will purchase the property. They used TV personalities to promote a free seminar where they would promote their first paid offer.

The plaintiffs accused the defendants of giving misleading earnings claims. They said that most customers who purchased these programs didn't make any money even though they were given the impression that they would.

The defendants were accused of misrepresenting what customers would get from their products and services, such as offering funding real estate deals and connecting them with cash buyers. They were also accused of encouraging customers to increase their credit card limits in order to pay for their programs.

Violations of the Telemarketing Sales Rule and Utah state law were cited, mainly regarding the misrepresentations discussed earlier.

Raging Bull

Company: RagingBull.com, LLC
Date: March, 2022
Complaint: www.DONTSAYTHAT.com/ragingbull

Settlement:
$2.4 million, which will be refunded to customers. Promises to end misleading income claims, get affirmative approval from consumers for subscription sign-ups, and provide them with a simple method to cancel recurring charges. Permanent injunction on one of the company's "gurus."

Summary:
Raging Bull sold stock and options trading services online. According to the FTC, many of their customers were retirees, older adults, and immigrants.

There were multiple claims against Raging Bull. They were accused of violating the FTC Act by giving misleading implied earnings claims. One way was by improperly using testimonials. The earnings claims made in the testimonials were not independently verified. They were also not a typical result of their customers.

The FTC claimed that RagingBull made frequent explicit and implicit earnings claims but did not have adequate substantiation to back up those claims. They had disclaimers that the FTC deemed inadequate.

Another accusation was misrepresenting the success of its instructors. For example, the FTC claims that one of the most prominent instructors consistently lost money in the stock market but made most of his money from subscription fees to Raging Bull.

The FTC criticized their refund policy. They claimed refund requests were regularly denied, and customers were encouraged to try a different Raging Bull service instead. Raging Bull was accused of delaying responses to customers trying to cancel recurring charges, resulting in some customers getting charged unexpectedly.

Response Tree

Company: Response Tree LLC
Date: January, 2024
Complaint: www.DONTSAYTHAT.com/responsetree

Settlement:
$7 million judgment. Suspended based on their inability to pay. Defendants are banned from making or assisting anyone else in marketing robocalls or calls to phone numbers on the FTC's Do Not Call Registry.

Summary:
Defendants generated leads for their customers. They primarily obtained these leads by operating websites where prospects disclosed their personal information, which was then sold to third parties.

The FTC claims that the defendants misrepresented the leads they sold to their customers, specifically the level of consent they received. The FTC also accused them of falsifying metadata to misrepresent where the leads were generated from.

Many of these leads were on the Do Not Call Registry.

The defendants were accused of violating the Telemarketing Sales Rule by collecting and contacting the leads and, by selling these leads, assisting and facilitating violations of the Telemarketing Sales Rule.

Russell Dalbey
Company: DEI, LLLP
Date: May, 2011
Complaint: www.DONTSAYTHAT.com/dalbey

Settlement:
Judgment of $330 million, which will be suspended when the defendants surrender their assets. Defendants were banned from telemarketing, selling business opportunities, and producing or distributing infomercials.

Summary:
The defendants sold products or services that taught customers how to find, broker, and earn commissions on seller-financed promissory notes. These are privately held mortgages or notes secured by the property subject to the loan. They were best known for the infomercial titled "Winning in the Cash Flow Business."

The FTC accused the defendants of making false claims, giving the impression that customers were likely to take advantage of this opportunity and make substantial amounts of money. The defendants were also accused of misrepresenting how successful the company's owner was in earning money from promissory notes.

Violations of the Telemarketing Sales Rule were an important part of the case. The defendants were accused of misrepresenting their offer and the results customers could expect.

Colorado state law violations were alleged in the complaint, mainly for the reasons already stated.

Tax Club
Company: The Tax Club
Date: January, 2013
Complaint: www.DONTSAYTHAT.com/taxclub

Settlement:
$255 million judgment, suspended after surrendering over $15 million in assets; specific bans on selling business coaching and work-at-home opportunities.

Summary:
The Tax Club sold tax preparation and advice, business planning and counseling, and business credit development services.

The FTC and the states of New York and Florida accused the defendants of misrepresenting the likelihood of recuperating their investment. They even implied that they could transfer the costs of purchasing the product to their future business.

The defendants were also accused of not delivering on the services that they promised, including unlimited access to tax and business advisors, along with the creation of personalized business plans.

Telemarketing practices were a major part of the case. The plaintiffs accused Tax Club of not properly introducing themselves at the start of the call, employing high-pressure sales tactics, and falsely claiming to be affiliated with companies from which consumers had already purchased products or services.

The plaintiffs also criticized Tax Club's refund policy. Tax Club offered full refunds within 3 days of purchase and partial refunds within 15 days of purchase. However, their services were not delivered within those time frames.

Violations of New York and Florida state laws were also alleged.

Vision Online (Ganadores)
Company: Vision Online, Inc
Date: June, 2023
Complaint: www.DONTSAYTHAT.com/ganadores

Settlement:
Judgment of $29,175,000. Over $6 million in assets were turned over to partially suspend the judgment. Several defendants were banned from selling ecommerce or real estate coaching services. Prohibition of certain business practices.

Summary:
Under the Spanish brand Ganadores Online, the defendants sold business opportunity programs to Spanish-speaking customers. These programs focused on selling third-party products on Amazon. They claimed their system didn't require significant money, good credit, or legal immigration status to succeed.

The FTC accused the defendants of using false and unsubstantiated earnings claims and other misrepresentations.

The FTC accused the defendants of pushing customers to take on significant credit card debt, claiming that customers would quickly recuperate their investments. The defendants also claimed that they provided customers with important documents in English, a language that many of them didn't understand.

The FTC also claimed that refund requests were regularly rejected. The defendants were accused of only offering partial refunds if complaints were posted on the Better Business Bureau and only if they removed those negative comments.

Vision Solution Marketing

Company: Vision Solution Marketing, LLC
Date: May, 2018
Complaint: www.DONTSAYTHAT.com/visionsolution

Settlement:
$15.15 million judgment. It was partially suspended after the defendants surrendered certain assets, including the remaining funds in their bank accounts. The judgment also bans defendants from selling business coaching or development services.

Summary:
Vision Solution Marketing sold products and services to help customers start home-based Internet businesses. It also offered business coaching services, many of which were sold through telemarketing calls.

The defendants were accused of false earnings claims. The FTC claimed that they directly or indirectly claimed that customers who purchased their coaching program were likely to earn substantial income even though most customers did not.

In addition, the FTC claimed that the defendants misrepresented what customers would get by purchasing the business coaching program. They were specifically accused of inaccurately stating that the program was only available to select qualified participants and that they would get personalized training and guidance from coaches.

The defendants were also accused of misrepresenting the need for their customers' financial information.

The complaint featured violations of the Telemarketing Sales Rule. These ranged from misrepresentations about the product to false statements to induce customers to sign up for the service.

Wealth Press

Company: Wealth Press, Inc
Date: January, 2023
Complaint: www.DONTSAYTHAT.com/wealthpress

Settlement:
Defendants had to turn over more than $1.2 million to the FTC to refund consumers. They also paid a $500,000 civil penalty. Requires defendants only to make earnings claims if they have written evidence to back up those claims. Also, defendants need to inform consumers about the case.

Summary:
WealthPress sold services around making financial transactions.

The FTC accused them of deceiving its consumers with false claims about the earning potential of its investment advising services, such as making over $24,000 every week without any market knowledge or trading experience. They used videos where they claimed to live luxurious lifestyles because of their successful trading strategies, which the FTC claimed was misleading or untrue.

WealthPress was also accused of violating the Restore Online Shoppers' Confidence Act (ROSCA). The main violation was improperly selling their products using a negative option feature.

Appendix

Zurixx

Company: Zurixx, LLC
Date: October, 2019
Complaint: www.DONTSAYTHAT.com/zurixx

Settlement:
Judgment of over $111 million, partially suspended with $12 million for customer redress. Permanent bans on selling any real estate or business coaching programs. Also barred from certain business practices.

Summary:
Zurixx, LLC sold real estate investment coaching, including live seminars and telephone coaching. Their focus was on flipping houses. To boost their sales, they used celebrity endorsements, including the hosts of the popular HGTV show *Flip or Flop*.

The FTC and the Utah Department of Commerce Division of Consumer Protection (UDCP) alleged that Zurixx applied high-pressure telemarketing tactics. During those calls, the defendants allegedly made earnings claims, saying that customers could make tens or hundreds of thousands of dollars by flipping or wholesaling real estate using Zurixx's system. Defendants also claim that customers could get their real estate investments 100% financed regardless of credit.

The defendants are alleged to have applied high-pressure sales tactics at their seminars. According to the FTC and UDCP, presenters at the seminars encouraged consumers to open new credit cards to pay for the training.

FTC and UDCP also alleged that Zurixx required consumers who received refunds to sign agreements barring them from speaking with the FTC and other regulators, submitting complaints to the Better Business

Bureau, or posting negative reviews about Zurixx. This violates the Consumer Review Fairness Act.

Zurixx is also alleged to have not properly disclosed its refund policy, and many customers received only partial refunds.